To The Students
of Mars Hill,

You've been so
gracious in raising up
not only the school
but our hearts to call
us to grow

"Dan Allender insightfully calls us to listen to our children through the loud background noise of life. The next book you read on parenting should be this one."

—TREMPER LONGMAN III, professor at Westmont College
and author of *How to Read Proverbs*

How Children
Raise Parents

THE ART *of* LISTENING TO YOUR FAMILY

How Children Raise Parents

Dan B. Allender, Ph.D.

WATERBROOK
PRESS

HOW CHILDREN RAISE PARENTS
PUBLISHED BY WATERBROOK PRESS
2375 Telstar Drive, Suite 160
Colorado Springs, Colorado 80920
A division of Random House, Inc.

Details in some anecdotes and stories have been changed to protect the identities of the persons involved.

ISBN 1-57856-110-8

Published in association with the literary agency of Alive Communications, Inc., 7680 Goddard Street, Suite 200, Colorado Springs, CO 80920.

Library of Congress Cataloging-in-Publication Data
Allender, Dan B.
    How children raise parents : the art of listening to your family / by Dan B. Allender.— 1st ed.
        p. cm.
Includes bibliographical references.
        ISBN 1-57856-110-8
    1. Parents—Religious life.   2. Parenting—Religious aspects—Christianity.   3. Parent and child—Religious aspects—Christianity.   I. Title.
        BV4529.A45 2003
        248.8'45—dc21

                                                                                                2002156449

Printed in the United States of America
2003—First Edition

10 9 8 7 6 5 4 3 2 1

To my children:
Anna, Amanda, and Andrew

Contents

I'm a Parent

What Was I Thinking? What Was God Thinking?

I have never had more difficulty writing a book than with this one. The writing process has spanned hardships and losses, pressures and demands that seem greater than all the other periods of my life combined. But none of that explains the real war being fought to make sure this book is brought to fruition...

Like most truth when it is finally embraced, it seems inconceivable that I didn't recognize it long ago. The reason I have not allowed the writing of this book to flow is simple: I am not a good father. I desperately love my children, and I am very troubled by what I have failed to be as a parent.

Each of my three children loves me fiercely. We have a bond that I am convinced will last and will extend beyond my lifetime. And my unease is not born of the heartache I experience when I see my children at times make awful decisions that are mainly due to my own failures. I have delightful, good kids. And, primarily, I have my glorious wife, Becky, to thank for that gift.

It is not simply the issue of failure that has hindered my writing. It is something more intangible and heart-searing. I finally was able to name some part of this ache when a writer friend of mine, who has heard me complain for two years about this book, wrote in an e-mail what she thought was going on. She articulated what I knew was inside me but that I couldn't seem to voice:

> It must feel awfully unfair that people believe you should know and do all the things that you teach. Isn't what you have taught—it is out of our weaknesses that we can speak? His strength is perfected in our weakness. So go for it. Yes, admit right off the bat, "I have no business writing this book because I am the chief of sinful fathers. There is no one worse than I. I have spent so much time teaching others that I have missed important moments in my children's lives: first word: ('da-da'), first T-ball game, kindergarten graduations, first dates.... When I have been 'with' them, I have often not been present. When I have been present, I have raged at them like a banshee.
>
> "But even more painfully, I must admit that there have been brief shining moments, when God's glory has broken through the dark clouds of my fury at my own painful childhood, and I have been the father the Father has called me to be. And those moments call me forth, make me ache as the barren woman in Isaiah 54 to labor and bear fruit in my children's lives. And yes, it is that place from which I write."

Those thoughts were stated by a friend when I couldn't put them together for myself. And they are true. Just as we must put words to our experience in order to be heard by another, we must also be read by others if we are to fully know our own hearts. So, like the psalmists, I have taken the words of another and used them as my own, because I long to be more than I am.

This book is primarily for parents. The doorway to knowing ourselves and God is often found in a relationship with someone who is dependent on our care. In such a relationship of need, we face how much we are given to give away to others as well as how often we do not give all that we have. It is that disparity between the potential and the actual that can break our hearts. I have so much; I give so little. There is no relationship on earth in which we are called to be more noble and to sacrifice more deeply than with our children. And our hearts are pierced more profoundly in that failure to give all than they are in perhaps any other relationship.

Why is this good news? Because no other arena in life holds us more hostage to hope, more afraid to dream, more defensive about our decisions, and more open to receive help—all simultaneously. The intensity and passion of parenting bring the potential not only for our worst, but also for our very best as human beings. It is the space in our lives where we are most open to the work of God to change us—if we will only allow our children to lead us into spiritual maturity.

I have one desire for this book: that we will fall more in love with our children and with the God who shows himself to be the divine, all-loving Parent whom we all hunger for. May you experience God's incredible, tender love as we learn about how our children raise us. May we all be amazed at how well God has written into the lives of our children just what we are meant to know about him.

Children Shape Our Souls

That's Why We Need to Read Our Kids

And the Child became Father to the Man.

—WORDSWORTH

The process of parenting continues to be the most haunting and holy experience of my life. It is unique in its unexpected foreignness. In contrast, my marriage is an up-and-down roller coaster of sorrow and joy, mostly deep joy; but it is a relationship I already knew something about before I entered it. Oh, I realize now that what I knew at first about my wife was in fact very little and mostly obscured by my own biases. But it was enough to get me into marriage and has been the basis of rich wonder and marvelous confusion as my views of my wife have changed over twenty-four years.

On the other hand, I did not choose my children. Instead, I chose to become a father. With each of my three children, I had no choice as to their gender, eye color, intelligence, aptitudes, health, or disposition toward life. They came fully formed and uniquely stamped.

What I knew about being a father could have been written several times over on the head of a pin. I knew it was a right thing to do. And now and then, at peculiar moments, I *wanted* to be a parent. In actuality, however, if my wife hadn't been so excited at the prospect of being a mother, I might have let the thought go until we had paid off more of our debts, purchased a little larger home, acquired just a few of the toys I'd always wanted, and matured enough to be a really good father. The last issue was the killer.

I was an only child who grew up with a mother who was herself an only child, which means I had no cousins, let alone siblings. I don't recall holding a baby or even being around a young child until I was in my twenties. This lack of familiarity was a significant but not central issue. More vexing was my self-centeredness. I had adored the privilege of being the only child in the house on Christmas to open the mound of gifts waiting under the tree. Family schedules were attuned to my life and no other. The family's resources were at my disposal, and I never needed to share anything.

Once I got married, I was smart enough to realize that if Becky and I gave birth (yes, I am aware of how absurd the word *we* is) to a little intruder, I'd be deposed from my throne. Even before we had children, though, life had changed because my wife would have nothing to do with me posing as her "only child" whether we had kids or not. I'd already been invited to give up my selfishness. Still, I knew a child would not only knock me completely off my throne, but would actually *take my place* on that throne. I was open to the prospect of parenting, but I wasn't going to be overly hasty about jumping into the water.

As Providence would decree, by the time I was ready to have children, we had suffered the travails of infertility and miscarriage. This chapter of our life was agonizing. The child my wife so desperately desired took over our sex life, consumed our free time, and sapped our hope every month when menses returned to mock our (my) impotent labor.

Tests were done. Temperature was measured. Prescribed moments of intimacy replaced spontaneity, and the rote task of conceiving began to deflate the passion of our intimate union. Sex became a job. The pregnancy dawned, and our exile was over only to have our hope denied in miscarriage. Something in me said, "Never again. I will never care enough about the merger of a sperm and an ovum to suffer that kind of pain again."

But I did. Another year passed, the fullness of my wife began and held, and over the following nine months we worried and fretted our way to the time Becky finally said, "This is the day. We need to go to the hospital." I jumped out of bed, grabbed my clothes and camera bag, and ran to the garage—only to realize that I wasn't dressed, I didn't have my keys, and my wife had not gotten out of bed. I eventually returned to bed, and three hours later, after fitful, terrified half slumber, we rose to go to the hospital.

The day is a blur.

After an agonizing process (the story will be told in a later chapter), I gazed at my infant daughter and was swallowed by something that is impossible to explain: I was instantaneously in love. Never in my life, other than at the birth of my other two children, have I been so completely and thoroughly caught up in the passion and glory of life. If someone that instant had demanded I give my life for my child, it would have been the one most completely selfless and effortless act of my life.

My first lesson—and how can it be called that without trivializing the moment?—was that a love existed in me that was raw, pure, and ferocious. My daughter's dark, delicate eyes consumed me in their beauty. I was besotted. But what infused me with such overwhelming love just at that moment? I was not so surprised by instantaneously loving my daughter, but I was stunned by its magnitude. I was *invaded* by love, a love that felt both alien to and exactly like me, but a me that I'd never considered myself to be. All of that came at the same instant that my thoughts were lost in my infant daughter's gaze.

It dawned on me at that moment: This child and my children to come will teach me more than I could possibly hope to ever teach them. Since that moment my life has never been the same. It never will be the same for all eternity, and I have my children to thank.

Here is the core premise of this book: Thank God for your children because they are the ones who grow you up into spiritual maturity. Far more than being concerned about how to correct, or convert, or counsel your children, thank God for what your children are teaching you. To the degree that your heart is overwhelmed with gratitude for your children, they will gain the core education they most need—the knowledge that they are truly loved, treasured, and delighted in. Only a genuinely thankful parent can invest in his or her children the conviction that they are the focus of unconditional love.

There is one slight problem, however. There are many, many times I am not grateful for my children. I suppose in some really big ontological, metaphysical sense, I am grateful even at those moments. At our core, most parents are deeply grateful for our children. But it only takes one fretful night of vomiting, a suddenly due Sunday-night science project, a lie, a shoplifting incident, a crisis pregnancy, or a child's determined flight from God to cause us to forget our gratitude. When our children shame us, it is far easier to be detached. At worst, it is possible to turn against them with blame, anger, and even rejection.

What Were We Thinking?

Most of the time we are grateful for our children without being particularly aware of it. There are other times when our joy and gratitude beam in full splendor. And then there are times when we ask ourselves, "What were we *thinking?*" At the outset, most of us don't consider the emotional and spiritual cost of being parents. And even if we were able to ponder the price, it would be impossible to fathom the kind of journey we were embarking on.

After our first bundle of joy was born, the most complicating reality Becky and I faced was how to move all the paraphernalia—car seat, stroller, diaper bag, toys, and clumsy video apparatus from home to our various destinations. These are mere logistical bumps in the road, and small bumps at that. Most parents can't even begin to imagine how their children will change them all the way down to the core of who they are. I know I never suspected it.

A few years ago I had the privilege of speaking at a crisis pregnancy fund-raiser and heard an amazing story about a father being transformed through his daughter. At the time I was exhausted with my kids and weary with life. As is often the case when I want to quit, God offers me a fresh vision and new hope through another person's story. This particular story turned my heart from the question *What was I thinking?* to a new question: *What is it, God, that you want?* That day at the crisis pregnancy center, I heard the life-transforming story of a wonderful, miraculous, ordinary man named David. I haven't been the same since.

David grew up in the South before the full advent of the civil rights movement, and segregation was a way of life. He attended a separate school, drank from whites-only water fountains, and went to movies in a theater that required the black kids to sit in a rickety balcony while the white boys and girls were seated on the main floor. That was simply the way things were.

His life followed a course typical for his social class. He went to college, got a good job, and had a family. Somewhere along the way, David's wife began to help out at a crisis pregnancy center. He was supportive, but he had his own world of commerce, church, and golf. He only occasionally joined his wife in her pro-life ministry.

Eventually she became director of the center. Conversations at the family's dinner table were seasoned with joyful stories of lives saved, as well as heartbreaking accounts of families ruptured and the tragic progression of various sexually transmitted diseases. It might not have been normal, middle-class dinner conversation, but the entire family was becoming engaged in the pro-life effort.

One day David's wife called and asked him to come to the center. When he arrived, his wife told him that their teenage daughter was pregnant. David was devastated. When he learned that the father was African-American, he became enraged. His daughter had not merely ignored God's prohibitions against premarital sex, but she had crossed a cultural line, violating a social taboo ingrained in him from childhood.

Suddenly the decision as to whether to take the pregnancy to full term was far more difficult than expected. But once that decision was reached, the issue of putting the baby up for adoption was unthinkable. The pregnancy progressed, and the day of birth came. David was there, and he looked into the eyes of his grandson soon after he was born.

Instantly, he fell in love. Or perhaps, more accurately said, love fell upon him. David told an audience of six hundred people that he immediately realized that his grandson was part of his flesh and blood. His grandson was black, so the new grandfather was black as well. A white man who had grown up in the segregated South and later had supported the integrated South, but without conviction or repentance, became in a single moment a black man at heart.

Tears rolled down David's face as he spoke. I looked around the room of southern men and women and saw hundreds of people in tears. There were also pockets of faces that were tense, stern, and struggling to remain polite. To those people David was marking himself as an alien and a stranger. And the alien was wet with joy over his grandson.

I don't know if I have ever felt the gospel to be more scandalous and beautiful than in those moments. David ended his talk by expressing gratitude to his daughter, who was sitting at the head table. He said, "I don't know how to thank you enough. You took a comfortable and sincere Christian man and tossed him into the arms of God. I've come back a man who knows his own sin and the love of God in such a way that I will never be the same."

David didn't use this phrase, but it would have been entirely consistent for him to do so: "You grew me up. You raised me to know God." It is our children who serve as the doorway we pass through to meet God face to face.

What Is God Thinking?

When are we grateful for our children? When do we delight in them, unable to contain our happiness and sense of being blessed? More often than not it's when they show the fine genetic disposition they were granted by scoring well on a test or sinking a fade-away jump shot just as the buzzer sounds. When our children fulfill our dreams and satisfy our expectations, we are aglow.

But when your son returns from a weekend visit to his older brother's house and shows you a new tattoo, the glow is doused. Or when your daughter brings home her new boyfriend and he's of another race, then it's a whole different story. Our gratitude is easily disrupted by surface issues that simply don't matter, or by issues that matter only to us parents in some private, life-preference way, but not at all to our children's well-being.

One problem is that we are too child driven. We spend too much money and time on child-oriented things that compete with the simple and profound appreciation we should feel for our child. In turn, the money and time we spend dragging kids to tennis tournaments, music lessons, debate club, and a legion of other devilish opportunities fuels a child's sense of entitlement and a parent's feeling that his child is an excessive drain on energy, time, and money. This sense leads to the attitude, "My kid owes me big-time."

There has never been an era when parents have spent more time, money, and energy on pleasing their children. And there has never been an era when children, in return, have shown their parents less respect, intimacy, and honor. Sadly, we are apt to blame our children for this. But there is very little responsibility that an eight-year-old, or a sixteen-year-old, or a twenty-two-year-old bears for her parents' failure. It's time for us to take responsibility for our own failure to be the kind of people who are good parents.

The first step toward a solution is to acknowledge that our focus is off. If one surveys the wealth of—actually, the *glut* of—videos and study guides and conferences and magazine articles on parenting, the focus is almost always on what to do with your child, not what it means to become a good parent. Engaging in more child-focused activities makes us feel as though we are improving, even as it deepens our resentment toward our children.

Among these parenting resources, we often find a list of generally agreed upon character qualities: honesty, fairness, consistency, care, compassion, empathy, love, commitment, and strength. No one should fault a single item on the list. But how helpful is it, really, to be told that we need to conform to these attributes and that we need to insist that our children do likewise?

When I ask adults what it takes to be a good parent, they parrot the psychobabble of the therapeutic field or the latest feeding schedule and spanking technique advanced by a more conservative wing of the parenting movement. Then they might toss in a dose of Rush Limbaugh or Homer Simpson, depending on which pop culture icon they spend more time with. But when I ask parents what they have *learned from their children,* their faces go blank. Even more, when I ask, "How have your children changed, transformed, redeemed your life?" I get a suspicious stare, as if I'm dressed in a seventies-era, pale green polyester leisure suit.

Why is it so hard to believe that God intends our children to train us just as much as he intends us to train and guide our children? Why is it so inconceivable that God would design a child to be the best qualified human to thwart and shatter a parent's arrogance and self-righteousness? And why don't we put this responsibility to learn on a par with the parent's responsibility to rightly shape the heart and mind of a child?

If we want to be good parents, we must learn to read our children. And that requires learning how to listen to our children—one of life's most difficult, most demanding tasks. To the degree that we read our children as God wrote them, we will grasp the ineffable glory of what we are most meant to know and enjoy. God intends to reveal himself to us through our children as much as, if not more than, he intends for us to teach our children about him. Unless a person—especially an adult—has the faith of a child, he or she will never enter the kingdom of God.[1]

What a radical claim! Unless we approach Jesus as a child, we have no hope of inheriting the kingdom. To meet Jesus as a child, we must be as needy, demanding, and immature as a child. Children are not noted for their profound grasp of the long run, nor their capacity for naturally putting aside immediate pleasure for the prospect of greater pleasure later on. Children are not skilled in relational complexity—reading motives, discerning schemes, shifting alliances—so they exhibit greater honesty and openness about what is simple and true. A naked emperor is still naked no matter how much money and time was spent weaving his illusions. We must approach Jesus with naked honesty and need, and there is no one better qualified to show us the way than our children. They are the expert guides we need if we ever hope to brush up close against God.

Let me make this claim at the outset: A change in our perspective will not only increase our joy and freedom in parenting, but in the long run it will invite our children to become coheirs of eternal life. And it will accomplish these things without us loading on the baggage and burdens that we often wrongly compel our children to carry. It will not only free us to have more fun as parents, but it will also allow our children to be more effective shapers of our souls. It's the most appealing win-win arrangement I can think of.

If you are a young parent or an expectant parent, you are likely feeling some apprehension about the twisting road that lies ahead. I want you to know that God has already set up a system that will relieve your fear and arm you with confidence. If you are an experienced parent, even one whose children have already left home, this book has just as much to say to you. A parent is never not a parent—even if you have teenagers whom you hardly ever see or grown children with kids of their own. They may leave your hearth, but never your heart. A new and exciting era of parenting awaits you not only with your young-adult children, but also with your grandchildren when they arrive. We are most alive and ready for transformation when we learn to listen to our children, and it's never too late to learn.

Let's turn the page and begin the listening process.

CHAPTER I

Listening to the Voice of Your Children

How to Answer Their Two Crucial Questions

A ging is inevitable, while becoming mature is uncertain. Our bodies grow from infancy to old age in a mere eight decades. This process of physical growth, however, is not always matched in the inner person. Some die when they are old without having truly advanced beyond adolescence. Others die young with souls having gained a weight and a depth that far exceeded their years.

Growing up, as opposed to merely growing old, compels us to embrace both joy and sorrow. To mature we must learn to suffer and not yield or turn hard. To mature we must also learn to engage joy and not demand that it hang around, nor fabricate a counterfeit when it departs. There are many other ways to measure maturity, perhaps, but they all dance to the music of sorrow and joy.

How we embrace—or refuse to hold—sorrow and joy will define our lives. If we capitulate to sorrow, we will become cowards. If we allow sorrow to make us hard, then we will grow cold and eventually cruel. If we demand that joy remain constant, we will become self-consumed. And if we create a counterfeit joy, our lives will be riddled with impulsivity and addictions. Life demands that we either grow or stagnate. As difficult as it is to face this truth regarding my own life, it is harder for me to grasp regarding my children. I know I must suffer, struggle, grow, and sometimes fail to mature. But when this reality shows itself to be just as true for my children, I can barely endure it.

The Voice of Sorrow

I heard the sound of muffled tears coming from my sixteen-year-old daughter's room. The door was closed, and her CD player tried to provide a cover for her pain. But when the music quieted between songs, I could hear her crying. My ear was pasted against the door, as it is whenever I fear that some harm is threatening one of my children. (Try to picture my oldest daughter's shock and disdain on another occasion when, after secretly plotting either the overthrow of the government or a clandestine rendezvous with friends, she opened her door to see her unbalanced father topple to the floor. If you are spying, don't lean against your child's door.)

As the sobs continued, I stood against my daughter's door, frozen and uncertain. Should I knock? Should I wait and ask about her day later at dinner? Should I go off somewhere and pray, get busy with some task, or simply try hard not to worry? Why doesn't someone tell me exactly what to do? I know enough to love my children, provide boundaries and consequences, and be patient with them. But what am I to do with tears? Do I let her work it out on her own, or do I boldly enter where no man, especially a father, has gone before?

I knocked, and there was silence. The music continued, but the tears dried up at the first sign of a potential intruder. When the intruder knocked again, my daughter answered the door, furious at being interrupted. A quick look told me everything. She was in pain, and she didn't want help. I was now the issue, and it was best to disappear. But as I do when I'm skiing, I had already aimed the pointy ends downhill, and due to certain forces of nature, I was fully committed. I was headed down the slope no matter what my daughter did or said.

I don't know what your parental default mode might be, but mine, whenever in doubt, is to state the obvious. "I heard tears," I began. "The door was closed. You are now not crying, but frowning. I know privacy is more important to you than food. You are now grimacing, and your lower lip is jutting out farther than your nose."

That last remark turned the tide. She broke, slightly. A smile rose and then departed like the winter sun in Seattle. But for a brief moment, a glorious moment, we made connection, and she let me stand in the doorway as a person, not merely as a parent.

I was never invited in, but I did hear a sketchy outline of a run-in with two of her girlfriends that had humiliated her in front of a guy she liked. Perhaps I wasn't invited into her room because she could see the fury rising in my eyes. I knew both of the friends in question, and I wanted to corner them in some public place and give them a taste of the same poison they had fed my daughter. How dare they hurt her after all the times she had stood beside them as they suffered with parents, boyfriends, school, and other calamities of life!

I'd rather take a bullet than see my children suffer. But I can't. I can protect them at some points, but those moments are too few and much too far between. Often, in fact, my efforts to warn them of impending danger or even to jump in front of the oncoming train actually intensify their suffering and intrude on the process of their maturing. So when do I jump to protect them, and when do I stand back and, in anguish, just watch and wait? I want answers and solutions!

There are times when I can't do anything other than offer a heroic gesture, no matter how futile; and there are other times when I can easily do something, yet I must stand back and let the process play itself out. I want my children to mature; I just don't want them to have to mature through suffering. But you can't have one without the other.

The Voice of Joy

There were eight minutes left, and our team was down 12 to 4. My seventh grader, Andrew, was the second-team goalie on the middle-school lacrosse squad. We were playing in the district finals, and the winner would go on to the state tournament. We had beaten this team before, and the match was intense and exciting. But for some reason our team was sluggish and nervous. As the game began to wind down and it looked hopeless, my son was sent onto the field. The home crowd began chanting his name: "Andrew, Andrew, Andrew…" Each time his name rose, my stomach tightened. He was going against a first-class squad that wanted to run the score to the high heavens at the expense of not only our team, but now also my son.

The first attack of the goal came within a minute after Andrew entered the game. The shooters worked the ball downfield, and I could see my son's body tense and his eyes widen. The first throw was hurled at his head. The hard lacrosse ball was a blur, and I involuntarily closed my eyes and held my breath. When I opened my eyes again and breathed, I saw that he had deftly caught the ball in his goalie stick and was throwing it to a teammate. The crowd roared. I could see his breathing slow down and his face relax. Then I looked at the clock and realized I would have to watch this spectacle for another seven minutes.

It is one of the oddest components of life. We want to succeed, and we feel something like joy when we are successful. Yet if we're convinced that joy is based on performance, we'll feel more and more pressure to always succeed. And the greater the pressure, the more likely we are to fail. In this way, joy intensifies sorrow.

The game proceeded, and the minutes slowed to a crawl. Andrew turned away six attacks, and finally they scored on him. He had played better than the first-team goalie, yet he had allowed a score. Now he was caught between the pleasure of playing well and the sting of his team's loss. When the game ended, many congratulated him on his fine performance. But when I put my hand on his shoulder, he shrugged it off. He didn't want his father touching him in front of his friends, and I suspect he didn't want anyone to touch his glory and either take a portion of it or disturb the fragile mantle he was wearing.

Once we got into the car, I didn't know what to say. I had told him that he played well and that I was proud of him. I asked what the coach had said ("Nothing much"). I so wanted to join his joy, but he persisted in holding onto it without my intrusion. I felt isolated and hurt. Why don't the experts tell us that we will feel lonely and alone, envious and jealous, confused and angry over our children's successes and failures? Or is it only me?

How Children Raise Parents

As difficult as it is to see our children grow up, it is a stroll in the park compared to being grown up by our children. To be a parent is one of the most terrifying, thrilling, overwhelming, and joyful experiences of life. It is the place where we become adults (if we are ever to be so) as we experience the most remarkable and unusual gift of life—being grown up by our own children.

There is no question about our parental responsibility to raise our children. We are older, wiser, and more experienced. The bruises of life have prepared us to see beyond the current calamity or the short-lived, yet exuberant, success. We parents must be our children's elders, coaches, counselors, mentors, cheerleaders. In other words, we parents must parent.

However, to be *great* parents, we must allow our children to shape our lives. We must not only guide and shape our children, but we must also go to them as students of life. If we will allow it, our children will grow us up to be mature adults who can offer them a taste of heaven. Thus the blessing is bestowed on both.

Becoming great parents is a learning process—it does not involve our following a list of rules. But to succeed in this learning process, we must let go of two pervasive myths: We must let go of the myth that right influence guarantees the desired results, and we must discard our unswerving faith in the power of right principles to guarantee success. This learning process requires a change in our practices and also a shift in our beliefs—neither of which is easy. But it's entirely possible if we keep in mind that our children raise us and, in so doing, make it possible for us to raise them well.

Examining and Discarding the Myths

We all share a central goal: parenting our children in such a way that they will become God-honoring, self-sacrificing, loving, and productive adults. However, in working toward this goal, we have to first dispense with the two myths that steal power from our parenting. Let's look first at the myth that says right influence guarantees the desired results.

DOES RIGHT INFLUENCE REALLY GUARANTEE DESIRED RESULTS?

We assume that if we give our children a "good" home—love, positive experiences, discipline, a quality education, and sufficient opportunities for success—they'll pass through childhood to adolescence with few bumps. We expect a good home life to move our children through college to marriage, family, career, church, and civic responsibilities with ease; and if not with complete ease, at least with sufficient confidence. We believe this process to be inevitable, the cause-and-effect relationship of responsible parenting that produces the well-adjusted and productive adults of tomorrow. That is, the results are inevitable if we can just keep our kids away from obstreperous peers, the pernicious media, and the sex and violence of the youth culture.

We cling to this "good influence" myth as if it were a promise from God, rather than seeing it as the religious wishful thinking that it truly is. The myth begins with the assumption that most middle-class homes have at least one parent on site, likely two, who will provide sufficient care and oversight to help children progress from childhood to successful adulthood; and not just successful adulthood, but a level of adult achievement that exceeds that of their parents.

This assumption is actually more cultural than it is biblical. It draws from cultural expectations that "good" parents provide their children with all the benefits the parents were given as children—*and more*. Our children will stand on our shoulders and climb the next rung on the ladder of upward mobility, or so the logic goes. If we do our part, it's virtually guaranteed that our kids will be brought to personal, social, and spiritual maturity by our hard work, prayer, and faith. Of course our efforts are bolstered by the positive influences of the social institutions we support—the educational system, church, Boy Scouts, music teachers, sports programs, and so forth.

It's difficult to argue against this assumption. On the surface, the power of good influence seems unassailable. Don't most children who are reared by caring, involved parents turn out well? Even those kids who go through rough periods in adolescence seem to eventually land full-time jobs, get married, and join the mainstream of productive citizenship. Parents make the sacrifice of leading responsible lives as their children grow up and then enjoy the reward of watching their children function as responsible adults. At least, we assume this cause-and-effect relationship holds true.

The research suggests, however, that parents are gullible if they assume that their influence and involvement will automatically produce the next generation of mature, productive adults. Sexual adventurism is on the rise. Violence is the number-one killer of adolescents after auto accidents. Cheating in school is viewed as an acceptable way to make the grade. Today's young adults are less apt to get married, and fewer young couples are having children. Less than 17 percent of those children raised in Christian homes end up attending church.[1] Our children require more than a stable home environment. If they are to grow into true maturity, we must go beyond the myth of inevitable influence.

Do Right Principles Really Guarantee Success?

All of this brings us to myth number two: our bedrock faith in the power of right principles. I admit, looking back at the way our parents raised us—especially if they were part of the World War II generation—would seem to prove the lofty promises of principled parenting. The much-admired Greatest Generation won a world war and then set about providing a secure environment and an educational system that prepared their sons and daughters either for college or a good career and families of their own. Our parents built their child-rearing model on solid principles, and in most cases it seems to have worked.

My parents were satisfied to keep me busy with healthy activities (and out of jail). They made sure that my homework was done, that I was involved in sports, and that I practiced my band instrument. Parenting was not rocket science, nor did it require a great deal of thought. It did require a steady hand and single-minded commitment to the goal of producing children who would achieve more than their parents had.

But that was then. Changing culture has made parenting a much more demanding and perilous calling. By almost every measure we live in a more dangerous world today. In the sixties suburban children didn't head off to school wondering if they would be gunned down by a classmate. Few eighth-graders met a friend at the movie theater anticipating group oral sex. Songs were not broadcast on the radio advocating the rape and murder of young women. But in our children's world, sex is devalued and violence is glorified. It's no mystery why our culture blesses cynicism. What alternative do we have?

Our culture continues to be in the throes of radical changes. The danger is high and the consequences of failure are overwhelming, so we demand that someone in authority tell us what to do. In times of chaos and uncertainty, sound principles do much to calm fears. Which of us right-thinking parents would not want to save our children from the scourge of our decadent world?

In response to that desire, the advocates of principled parenting offer a guarantee: If parents adhere to the right list of biblical principles mixed with a smattering of psychological insights, their consistent implementation of these principles will provide a child with the grounding to escape harm and to grow toward health and hope. Simply follow the principles, and you and your kids will succeed.

But does this guarantee hold even a drop of water? Life doesn't unfold in a straight line, and our children aren't computer programs. Parenting is far from a scientific pursuit; it's messy and risky and a huge leap of faith. Even the best set of principles can't answer the most important parenting question: "What do I really need to do to ensure that my children will turn out all right?"

Someone Has to Know What to Do!

Here's the guarantee that proves true: Read the Scriptures, and you'll find principles worth adhering to. But look for ironclad guarantees about how your children will turn out, and you won't find any. If anyone makes you such a promise, don't believe it.

Every time I walk into a bookstore, I check the parenting section to see what new works have appeared. I usually hunt first for books about dealing with adolescents. My children range from ages fourteen to twenty-two, and my interest in what experts have to say is not merely academic. I really do need help.

A recent "typical moment" in my family demonstrates my genuine need for help. I walked into the house from my garage office and overheard two animated conversations, indicating that my best course of action would be to retreat. My wife was exhorting my son, while my youngest daughter was bellowing at her older sister. If I'd been wise, I would have slid back out the door.

Andrew had not finished an English assignment. Annie, our oldest, had taken a pair of jeans from younger sister Amanda. Plus my wife was unhappy. Someone had forgotten to pick up the groceries, and there were four lists of chores for the children and the husband to finish before dinner would be put on the table. All I wanted just then was a snack, perhaps a brief chat, and then a quick return to my home office. But that was not to happen. The situation I'd walked into called to mind movie images of trench warfare from World War I. You know the scene: Enemy troops are advancing, making it dangerous for you to raise your head, either to go forward or to fall back. Yet it's not an option to stay put. Your position could be overrun at any moment. You're in a no-win situation, but you've got to do *something*.

I want to find the expert who has not only figured out how to make child rearing work, but has perfected it in his or her own home. That person can show me how to turn these unattractive moments of familial warfare into happy times of warm bonding.

Perhaps my kids need more discipline. Or maybe my wife and I need to take some of the pressure off so they can just be kids. Could it be that we haven't spent enough time praying for our children? We may need more quality time as a family, or maybe we haven't yet landed on just the right sport, musical instrument, or church youth group. Our situation demands the wisdom of an expert, not the muddled thinking of a mere parent.

Now let's return to reality. Most people know that no expert has a handle on the maze of issues facing every child, parent, and family. And a book containing good parenting principles is at best a picture taken from thirty thousand feet. It gives us a grand view of the terrain far below, but seldom does it provide a walking guide to choose one path over another when it really counts. When the smooth trail we've been on suddenly forks, and both options look equally steep and rocky, where are the principles that shout: "Take rocky trail A! And avoid rocky trail B at all costs!" Those are the principles I need but can't for the life of me locate.

Beyond Principles to the Process

When the skies are clear and everyone is happy and the kids are thriving, we feel as though we must be the smartest parents on the planet. It's when we get tangled in the middle of the thicket that we realize our limitations and cry out for *the solution.* A good first step toward that solution is recognizing that we have the advantage of broad principles and the tools, intuition, and prompting that God provides when we cry out for help. But there is yet another source of help that almost all of us completely overlook, and that is the expert we have close at hand, our child. We must not turn merely to sound principles, but to the *process* of learning from our children how to parent them. And the learning process begins with learning to hear their voices.

When I walked into the house from my garage office, my son was silent as his mother voiced her displeasure over his failure to finish a major school assignment. His face indicated that he was somber but not broken and that he had only minimal desire to finish the assignment. If there was regret, it seemed he was only sad that he'd been caught. What does it mean to listen to his voice (even when he was silent) and truly see what's in his heart that is being communicated through his face? His eyes were telling a story. His facial muscles were tense and full of unspoken anger.

Amanda's voice was shrill and rancorous when she accused her older sister of taking her jeans. Annie was defiant, unmoved by her sister's accusations. What does it mean to hear their voices? We must become better at hearing what is spoken behind the actual words being said. We must learn how to read our children's core questions, accusations, and invitations.

LISTENING FOR THE CORE QUESTIONS

Beginning with the first day of life outside the womb, every child is asking two core questions: "Am I loved?" and "Can I get my own way?" These two questions mark us throughout life, and the answers we receive set the course for how we live.

As a parent I am called to answer both of these questions not only accurately and continuously, but also simultaneously. Parenting is not difficult; it is impossible. How am I to answer both questions for Andrew when his faraway, disinterested gaze is registering now on other questions: "Can't I just do this homework later? Mom, why can't you finish the project for me? And anyway, why isn't it still summer vacation?"

It would not be all that difficult to veto Andrew's evening plans and make him finish the assignment. But is that what he needs most? Is it a matter of keeping him home, giving him a hug, and reminding him that we love him and are doing this for his good? The question "Am I loved?" is not easily answered by cheap words of solace. Truly listening to his voice, on the other hand, does not mean hearing how tired he is and how unfair it is to have all this work to do and then cutting him slack so he doesn't have to finish the assignment. To answer yes to his question "Can I get my own way?" would be cheap grace motivated by laziness or fear of answering him with a no, rather than true love for my son.

These two core questions are intended by God to compel us to face the deepest issues about the nature of life. A whining child may be asking, "Since I'm so tired, won't you do it for me?" It is also possible that the child really is asking, "Will you still delight in me if I end up blowing this test?" We can only discern the difference by learning to read our child's bent and allowing her to teach us what she most deeply needs from us at the moment. Furthermore, we must ask and answer the two questions about our own lives: "Am I loved?" and "Can I get my own way?" We can offer answers that are sure, rich, and deep for our child only if we know the answers for ourselves.

My failure to answer the two questions well for my children exposes my need to know and experience the answers more fully for myself. In fact, my child's accusation regarding my failure to answer well is meant to open my heart to hearing the voice of God. This is one way that my children help me mature into a true adult.

LISTENING TO CORE ACCUSATIONS

Despite what we saw earlier about guarantees, there is one guarantee about parenting: We all fail to answer the two core questions accurately and simultaneously. And when our answers veer off course, we become the targets of our children's accusations. Their words take us back to the need to really listen to them.

At times my son needs to hear clearly, "You can't get your own way," but I am lazy or too busy, and I ignore his voice. When I fail to answer, he learns that, at certain moments or in some areas, the rules of life don't apply to him and that, if he is patient and cunning, he can get what he wants. At times my daughter just needs a gentle touch on her shoulder and an acknowledgement that life can be hard. But there have been moments when I was too self-absorbed to answer that indeed she is loved, so I've told her to stop complaining and to get her work done. It's too easy to respond to our children's voices with answers to a question they didn't ask.

Perhaps even more common is our failure to address the question that is less overt. My younger daughter's rage about her sister taking her jeans is a classic example. Amanda was in a nasty mood and was spoiling for a fight. She wanted to be queen of the universe, but no one would bow down. A few moments of conversation with her exposed a raw disappointment from earlier in the day that was like a thorn festering in her paw. As soon as that thorn was plucked and the paw was bandaged, the borrowed jeans were traded for the opportunity to wear her older sister's leather skirt. Their interaction quickly became playful and kind. But Amanda's core question "Am I loved?" had to be answered first.

When we fail to hear their true question, we can't respond to our children's deepest desires. When we fail to listen, we do our children harm. That's when they generally respond with an accusation: "Why are you so angry and impatient with me? Why can't you be kind?" Consider the types of struggles that come to the surface when we fail to hear the real questions on our children's hearts.

Look at the chart to follow (Figure 1) that links our children's two core questions with the most common parental responses. The way we listen and respond to a child's voice leads to either the child's benefit or detriment. There are four options for answering the two core questions, but most parents answer in one of the three combinations that have detrimental effects. Only the fourth combination brings benefit.

Can I Get My Own Way?

		YES	NO
	NO	DANGEROUS/ DEMEANING	RULE-BOUND/ DULL
Am I Loved?	YES	INDULGENT/ DISTANT	STRENGTH/ DELIGHT

The Dangerous and Demeaning Response

Parents who regularly answer the two questions with "*Yes,* you can get your way. And *no,* you are not loved" raise children who learn that their parents don't care what they do and that their parents do not enjoy them. Because the parents are unwilling both to suffer the hardship of enforcing boundaries and to embrace the joy of truly loving their children, theirs is a soulless and inhuman home.

These parents fail to reflect both God's strength and his mercy. Children need to experience the strength of enforced boundaries and appropriate discipline as well as the mercy of being loved completely. The home that reflects neither aspect of God's character will either be actively abusive at one end of the continuum or, at the other extreme, the parents will be so uninvolved and emotionally removed that neither even notices when a child comes and goes.

The children in this home lack a conscience and have no concern for others. A boy will typically learn to survive on his wits; a girl often will get by on her body's assets. This is how we get macho, self-absorbed athletes and girls who get what they want by dispensing sexual favors. A child who grows up in such a home must find both love and rules elsewhere. Their search will usually lead to a gang or other group that serves as a surrogate family.

The Indulgent and Distant Response

Many parents answer "*Yes,* you can get your way" and "*Yes,* you are loved." Their children lack strength, and they grow up knowing only a counterfeit tenderness. These parents often are well-to-do, highly educated people who care more about public image and appearances than the hearts of their children. They dispense love through gifts, the provision of a nanny as a surrogate parent, or overprotective, overly possessive care. The children often are poised and competent, but they lack the strength of conviction and character that develops through bumping up against consistent boundaries.

The children in this family are likely to accuse their parents of being manipulative, since the parents are unwilling to embrace suffering and their joy is found outside the home. The children's accusations surface through acting out, getting in trouble, or pushing the limits to see if anyone will be strong enough to truly care. These children want the strength of appropriate discipline and long for the experience and delight of real love.

The Rule-Bound and Dull Response

Parents who answer no and no—"You *cannot* get your way" and "You are *not* our delight and joy"—often establish a conservative home characterized by stringent rules, clear consequences, and high demands on the children. At the same time, this home often lacks warmth, humility, laughter, and tears. The children perform well, obey the rules, and succeed through hard work and perseverance. What they lack is passion, whimsy, playfulness, and vision.

The children in this home accuse their parents of being self-righteous and dull. The parents are lacking in joy and are only too willing to suffer the discomfort of enforcing the rules. The children's accusations are made through silence and emotional distance. They see their parents either as gods or as cold, self-righteous despots. The children's response to such adults is to remain polite and disengaged.

The Response of Strength and Delight

This fourth option is the only correct answer to every child's two core questions: "*Yes,* you are loved beyond belief" and "*No,* you cannot get your own way." These two answers provide children with strength that watches out for their welfare and with the delight of being loved without conditions. Sadly, this combination is the least common among the answers today's children are receiving. Too many parents shun the discomfort and inconvenience that come with answering no to the second question. Meanwhile, the unwillingness to embrace joy keeps many parents from answering the first question with a resounding yes.

Our children hunger to know that they are loved unconditionally, through failure and success, no matter what they say or do. And, while few would ever admit it, they are dying to experience the security and comfort that come with appropriate boundaries. The best part of listening to our children as they continue to ask these questions is that they are inviting us to bring about positive change—in their lives and in our own.

The Questions Are Invitations

As our children ask the core questions, they are wondering about two additional matters: "What is wrong with my family?" and "How can I fix things?" All children unknowingly try to fix their mother and father and change the fabric of family life. If we were really listening, we'd hear the child's unspoken words as they attempt to provoke change. Our children invite us to grow, to become *fully human.* The invitation comes by way of unvoiced questions: "Will you cry with me? Will you hold me? Will you be strong enough to face your own failure and grow as my parent?"

Every child, by asking the two core questions, is offering an astounding invitation: "Will you love me and be strong? Will you provide a world where for a few, brief years I can experiment with passion and play and know that I can fail without losing your delight and joy?"

If we learn to listen to our children, we will find a precious truth: What they deeply crave is the same core desire we find in *our own hearts*. As we listen, we will learn to ask the same questions of the God who has made us and called us to be parents. We will ask him if he will still delight in us if we take great risks, discard some venerated rules, and sometimes fail miserably in our efforts to raise our children well. And we'll learn to listen to his answer to us: "*Yes*, you are loved more than you can ever fathom" and "*No*, you can't have your own way. But as you pursue *my* way, you will find the deepest satisfaction your heart can ever know."

CHAPTER 2

To Principles, Add Wisdom

The Solution to Formulas That Don't Deliver

Experts have scared the stuffing out of parents by implying that the challenge of raising children is too complex for a mere human to handle. The implication is both true and profoundly untrue.

It is true because God's call for a parent to imitate God[1]—reflecting his character in both perfect strength and tenderness—is impossible. Jesus is the tender face of the Father; he weeps over Jerusalem as a mother hen who wishes to gather her chicks safely under her wings.[2] In Jesus, God gently and passionately enters our human condition and yearns for us to return to his tender care. Jesus is also the face of God's strength in disciplining his beloved children, leading to righteousness and peace.[3] Jesus lived out both of these— strength and tenderness—perfectly, but human parents are not perfect. No matter how hard we try, we still stumble.

However, it's also quite *untrue* that the parenting task is impossible. I know this because God loves to empower us to do, or at least take a crack at, the impossible. Just think about the incredible things he commands us to do, including his calls for us to be holy and perfect.[4] Considering the high standards God establishes, it's odd that the Bible spends more time explaining how to prepare the sanctuary for ritual sacrifices than it does on how to promote godliness in our children.

This doesn't set well with our fix-it mentality. We want the easy step-by-step solution, and we want it spelled out in black and white. But God doesn't always operate that way. When it comes to the questions parents ask, the Bible is not a detailed instruction manual. Instead, it's a wild poetic history of God's engagement with fallen humanity. The Bible offers us principles on countless issues, including the admonition and nurture of children, yet there is precious little in the Bible on the finer points of parenting when things get really dicey. And ironically, that's exactly when we are the most desperate for clear-cut instructions.

Our fear of failure has fueled a mega-industry in parenting seminars, videos, satellite conferences, and magazine articles. The common theme running through these approaches is that if you do parenting "right," your kids will avoid the common pitfalls and turn out well. This promise rests on three presumptions: (1) The Bible lays out a detailed and comprehensive strategy for raising children, (2) the Bible promises a positive outcome if its principles are diligently followed, and (3) the Bible predicts that bad parents will produce bad kids. While widely accepted as gospel truth, all three presumptions are seriously flawed.

It is tragic that the Bible has been twisted into a self-help book when in fact it is silent on most matters confronting today's parents. Our consumer mind-set responds to such silence by inventing new principles and pretending they are part of the biblical canon. Sadly, these extrabiblical inventions impose rules and restrictions that God himself does not require. Such principle-directed parenting leaves us feeling guilty about exercising freedom and creativity, adapting approaches to fit our culture, and crafting a parenting approach that is "fit" to the uniqueness of each child.

If you listed every passage on raising children found in the Bible, you'd notice tremendous gaps. There is little about the stages of a child's development. There is little on how to discipline, when, or for what reasons. There is little on love and nothing on developing self-esteem, addressing peer issues, cultural engagement, or cultural disengagement. There is much on sexuality and nothing on developing a healthy body image.

The Promise That Isn't a Promise

Not only does the Bible fail to provide a comprehensive guide to parenting, but it also fails to promise that if you follow all the rules, your kids will turn out well. The passage most often cited as a guarantee to conscientious parents is Proverbs 22:6. In the New Living Translation it says, "Teach your children to choose the right path, and when they are older, they will remain upon it." The verse seems eminently straightforward and optimistic, if not exactly a money-back guarantee: Teach kids right from wrong and then hang on for a few years; as adults they'll practice everything you taught them.

That optimistic rewording, however, is a misreading of the text. In fact, the proverb is describing a way of approaching life rather than prescribing a formula that promises the desired outcome. The proverb invites us to teach our children according to each one's unique "bent," their natural inclination and learning style. And if we work in concert with our children's uniqueness, they won't depart from their God-given bent even as they age. If we were working with wood to fashion a bow for hunting, we would bend the wood in the way it is formed rather than to try to refashion it by bending it in the opposite direction. The wisdom of Proverbs 22:6 is to find and follow our child's natural bent. This is not a guarantee of success, but a practical guideline that leads to parenting well.

As Becky and I know from direct experience as well as from the experience of other parents, you can keep your children in Sunday school and then youth group until they turn eighteen, and the kids can still mess up their lives. Can we then assume that the child had "bad" parents? Often well-meaning folks point to 1 Timothy 3:4-5 where we're told that a person who aspires to be a church elder must "manage his own family well, with children who respect and obey him. For if a man cannot manage his own household, how can he take care of God's church?" The passage seems clear: If your kids are messing up, it proves that you don't know how to manage your home.

Perhaps the strongest antidote to that interpretation is to check God's own rate of success as a Parent. How did his Old Testament children turn out? God is the *only* perfect Parent, and even his wise skills and unconditional love failed to keep his children from rebelling. This is not an indictment of God; it is merely an acknowledgment of the folly of the children. God loved and disciplined his children; still, they chose the path of rebellion.

God managed the nation of Israel perfectly but failed to achieve the success we would expect. The word *manage* implies "providing care." In 1 Timothy 3:4-5, the message is simple: If a parent refuses to care for his own family, we ought not expect that he will serve, suffer, and sacrifice himself for the larger family of God. When you fail to serve your family, there will always be a higher probability that your children will neither respect nor obey you. But with the care provided by a self-giving parent, there is a higher likelihood that sufficient respect and trust will be developed and that the family will remain intact. Children who respect their parents also tend to take their parents' care and concerns seriously.

What we need is not a better list of principles, but godly knowledge that grows into parenting wisdom. *Principles* are the basics, like the alphabet and the multiplication tables of life. *Knowledge* is an understanding of the ways, means, and ends of God; it is the direction that biblical principles take us. Once we learn the basics, we then need to move toward wisdom. *Wisdom* is the creativity to apply principles in a real encounter with our children, when life's complexity refuses to conform to a simple rule. If knowledge is the how, then wisdom is the what, where, when, and why of parenting.

Wisdom always incorporates knowledge, but it adds intuition, experience, risk, and creativity. It is imperative to know the basics and then move on to practicing wisdom in life. The basics involve consistent discipline, which reflects God's strength, and constant care, which reflects God's mercy. Every child, no matter the age, needs to know limits and consequences (strength) and the tenderness of touch and the delight of a parent's eyes (mercy). Remember a child's two insistent questions: "Am I loved?" and "Can I get my own way?" Discipline and care begin to answer those questions in heart-touching ways. As parents act according to the twin principles of strength and mercy, they reflect the character of God into the lives of their children.

The ABCs of Discipline

Every child at any age wants to know where she fits in her parents' world: "Am I the center of the universe, and can I get what I want no matter what the cost to you, me, and others?" The loving answer to this question is "No!" because a child without discipline is destined for a living hell. If the right answer is so straightforward, then why do we see children (even adult children) demanding their own way and making life hell for those around them? Because answering the two core questions is hard for parents—it is frighteningly simple and simply frightening.

IT'S FRIGHTENINGLY SIMPLE

There are rules to be obeyed all through life. Like death and taxes, discipline specifies the limits of choice and then attaches a consequence to any violation. "If you don't put your clothes in the hamper, they will not be laundered." Or "If you keep screaming in the grocery cart, I will first put back every single item you chose. Then I will take away your television privileges tonight. If you fail to cease and desist, I will begin a discipline process that will include warming your rear end with a wooden spoon." This is always followed with the glorious phrase, "It's your choice."

It is simple to state a rule's parameters and the boundaries of choice: "You may not wear x, y, and z, but you can wear any other outfit and in whatever color combination you wish. If you choose to disobey, you will stay home with us and watch reruns of *Lawrence Welk.*" It is equally simple to create well-understood, onerous consequences that may not stop the behavior, but will usually slow the child down long enough to make the choice conscious and therefore culpable.

If parenting is this simple, then why aren't we enjoying the success that we'd expect? It's because setting limits and enforcing consequences is really inconvenient. If we state clear consequences, then when the line is crossed, we have to drop whatever we're doing. We have to make the arrest, read the little criminal her rights, transport her to jail, and give her time to plead her case. Once judgment is passed, we must apply the consequences and then bear the unpleasant aftermath. And it's not just the shrill complaining of the little lawbreaker. There will always be plenty of others—the offender's siblings, sometimes the grandparents, the other parent, neighbors, friends, people at church—who will question our methodology.

Since this is so much bother, we'd much rather just ignore the child's crime. Choosing the course of strength costs us way too much in time and trouble. But an even bigger issue that prevents consistent discipline is that we're afraid of our children.

IT'S SIMPLY FRIGHTENING

Every parent harbors one huge fear: that his or her child will break the parent's heart. Every child has the power to bless or curse a parent, and the difference between the two spells joy or shame. At a more basic level, I want my children to respect and like me. When it's clear for longer than about forty-five seconds that they don't respect me, I begin to panic. I've told all my children, "I am not your friend, and I don't care if you like me." And they all know that it's a lie.

The fear of losing a child's respect has a simple origin. If I am strong on enforcing boundaries, I will lose the intimacy and pleasure I so deeply missed with my own parents. That risk is too great, especially when the child's offense—the failure to brush teeth or pick up dirty clothes or tell the complete truth—doesn't seem like that big of a deal in light of the tension that will develop if I impose consequences. Of course, in light of the bigger picture, discipline is never an option. It's as important to the child as food.

The Bible says we doom a child if we refuse to provide clear boundaries and consequences. It further states that a child without discipline is unloved.[5] We may differ on how much time a child should spend on the computer or watching television, and what movies are acceptable, but we'd better have *some* rules, or we are killing our kids. Along with wise rules, we need appropriate consequences. Otherwise our empty rules are an invitation for the child to mock our authority. The best way to create an anarchist is to burden him with rules that are never consummated in a consequence.

Rules give a child the relief, confidence, and security that come from knowing there is someone stronger in the world than himself. When rules are enumerated but never enforced, it's like finding out there is no great wizard but simply a befuddled man hiding behind the curtain. Every child needs the comfort and consistent discipline of rules and consequences.

Beyond the strength of discipline, our children also need passion and delight—which leads to the answer to their other core question: "Am I loved?"

The ABCs of Mercy

The love that parents show to their children is a reflection of God's mercy. The basics of love include physical touch and the delight that parents take in their children. Again, it is so simple it's frightening. Children learn they are loved through the very earliest sensate experiences: They are warm and safe, and their stomach is full. It is through human touch that children are drawn close to the breast, changed, held, rocked, and lifted up to see the grand expanse of their world. Children also need to experience their parents' delight. They need to see their mother and father's faces, especially the eyes.

All children are meant to see the holy, wild joy of delight in the eyes of their parents. It is through touch and delight that children come to know they are desired and safe.

If love is this simple, why are millions of children neglected and abused, left starving for the care they so desperately need? I believe the two primary reasons are a parent's fear and envy.

FEARS OF THE NIGHT

The unknown is frightening. And nothing scares a parent more than knowing we have little influence and almost no control over the health, success, and life choices of our children. No matter what we do, a birth defect can mark our not-yet-born dream. Or a drunk driver can snatch away the life of our teenager. It is the fear of love that turns care into cold duty.

Many parents have been so scarred by the past that to open their hearts fully to a child is too dangerous. But they will do their duty and provide food, clothing, education, a warm bed, and watered-down love rather than the wild, uninhibited love that a child craves. Children who live in such a dutiful home know in theory that they are loved, but they never experience what it is to be loved. For them, love is simply provision; it is not touch and delight.

Parents fear the future—will my child prosper and live? Parents also fear the past—can I love now and risk hurt again? And often parents are far too involved in the demands of the present to offer a child a warm lap and the bright eyes of delight.

ENVY OF THE DAY

It is a dark and often unnamed fact that parents envy their children. We envy their youth, their fresh opportunities, and the freedom to have child-sized problems. We forget that a twenty-pound problem to a child who weighs sixty pounds is a third of her being, whereas the same problem to a two-hundred pound man is only ten percent of his reality. In any case, our problems and demands seem huge, when all our children have to do is get their homework done, clear the dishes from the table, keep the noise down, stop torturing their siblings, and brush their teeth. I know this because there are many days I wish I had my children's world. When I envy my son, it's usually when I am comparing my boyhood to his life. My childhood suffering seems more severe than my child's. It's hard to sacrifice for someone who has it so much better than I did.

Envy is not limited to the way we view our children. We see it also in our obsession with work. Why are we so afraid of losing our job or having to live on less money? It is always, at core, envy. It is envy that motivates all labor.[6] Yet often we don't have enough life left in us from our day at war (in the office or at the factory) to have much to offer. We're like walking zombies that dispatch the evening meal as fast as possible so we can slump into an easy chair to be carted off to another world through television.

Zombies don't do a good job reflecting God's mercy and delight. For zombies, caring for children is a rote duty. They must be fed, watched, disciplined, and driven to yet another lesson or event. It's not hard to see why children, missing out on hugs and expressions of delight, become a nuisance. Add to this the fact that many children disappoint their parents for no other reason than that they are normal, typical kids. They populate the large middle bulge of the bell curve, ranking right in average range. Most parents hate that. Surely a child who benefits from my genetic and nominative stature should rank ahead of most other children. We start to envy the other kids, those who seem to be above average, and again envy pollutes the ground of love.

Far too many parents refuse to face the truth that fear and envy sap the light of love out of their eyes and turn touch into a duty, not a delight. Fortunately, this can change. Knowledge demands that we face the truth about our fear and envy, then conform our lives to what is true. When we do, we begin to develop the groundwork for the growth of wisdom. A parent needs nothing less than knowledge, but far more than an assortment of principles. We must grow in wisdom in order to be strong and tender in ways that most peculiarly touch and delight our children.

Child-Oriented Wisdom

The ability to listen is the first component of practicing wisdom. We listen first to God and then carefully, patiently, to our children. Little in life is truly as it seems, and that is precisely why we need wisdom. The wise parent draws to the surface the matters of the heart and ascertains the pulse of what is not said, yet is loud enough to hear.

Wisdom helps parents assess the situation, determine strategy, and choose methodology. Will tenderness simply invite a child to wallow longer in weakness, or will a hard-line stand engender fear in a child? The wise parent can taste when the angry mood of a conversation is due more to a child's fear than to rebellion, and when a quiet and compliant spirit is more a flight from engagement than it is true obedience.

Here's a necessary irony: Those who are wise know they lack wisdom. One of the greatest marks of wisdom is the desire to grow wiser. It is the reason James wrote, "If any of you lacks wisdom…ask."[7] The wise know how easy it is to drift back and forth between ignoring and overreacting to our kids when they need either the strength of discipline or the mercy of tenderness. In asking God for wisdom we are more open to seeing our errors and hungrier to know what is true, good, and lovely. No one can parent well without wisdom.

It is wrongheaded to imply that I know how to develop wisdom. I am a poseur in these woods. But I do know where I have strained in prayer to gain wisdom. I have asked God repeatedly for help in four areas: clarity on how to read my children's unique bent, help to avoid majoring on the minors, depth of trust in him when things get tough, and the ability to live out surprise and paradox with my children. I suspect if we see growth in these key areas, we'll see it trickle down to other areas as well.

READING A CHILD'S UNIQUE BENT

In our highly psychological day, the concept of a person's "bent" is often defined as a personality pattern or style. Personality is a useful concept, though it is not identical to the concept of a bent. A bent is the manner in which God has uniquely written a person's life story to reveal God's character. It is closer to the idea of a theme or the deeper meaning of a story. Reading our children's bent is not a matter of taking a series of personality tests. Instead it is the demanding call to watch, listen, study, and interpret our children. It requires enormous wisdom to see our children's true bent versus our own dream for what our children will accomplish or become.

This task is not something to take lightly. I am to apply the best of my being to the bent of my child. It is a heady and holy, awesome and awful responsibility. How dare I name and shape the meaning of my child? How dare I risk his future by the many moments he will spend with me through his most formative years? At the same moment, I must not put the whole force of my being on my child, or I will crush him with my dreams and demands. I must follow not my own bent, but my child's God-given proclivities.

"But wait just a minute. Don't I know what my children need far better than *they* do?" How you answer that question will determine how you parent. If your answer is "Of course I know better than my child," then you will dictate your own life orientation to your children. This is how we arrive at rules such as dessert always has to come last and God deserves to see kids wearing a necktie rather than faded blue jeans on Sunday morning. I fear the harrumph of parents who assume they always know better than their children. But sadly, this assumption is the basis of much Christian parenting.

The same harrumph gives parents false confidence in the midst of life's confusion. It's an easy process to follow what seems to have worked for other parents and then pound away at it with your own children. Look at how things are done at your church or what the latest expert recommends. Soon your children will be toeing the line with the right clothing, schedule, after-school activities, and tastes in entertainment. It's just that simple, and it's simply a lie.

Life is not simple. That's why child-oriented wisdom includes the understanding that your child is meant to be in, but not of, the world. And that is not only the world outside the home, but the world *inside* the home. Each of my children is meant to be an Allender, but in the unique way that their first name marks each of them as an utter, complete individual.

Wisdom, the deep and abiding truth of God, must be the marrow in my bones if I am to know the difference between my own bent and the bent of my child. Is it me who longs to have a daughter who plays tennis and a son who fly fishes, or is it *their* bent? Is it my bent to want children who struggle deeply and surrender passionately to the wild God of the universe, or is it their bent to be moral, good-hearted humans who take a more "balanced" view of faith? How can my children grow to become who God created them to be when for years I am the largest shadow that towers over their life?

Wisdom cuts through the undergrowth of presumption and arrogance that characterizes all parents. Indeed, we *don't* know better than our children. Their bent is given by God, after all. Wisdom creates a poised openness that is willing to make decisions about our children ("You will play piano") while also relenting when it becomes apparent that there is a better fit elsewhere ("Or perhaps you're better suited to drama").

Not Majoring on the Minors

Wisdom helps us determine what really matters and what doesn't. Far too many power struggles are set into motion by a parent majoring on a minor issue while neglecting to address the major concern hiding underneath the bone of contention. It is possible to rail on a child for not getting his homework finished when the more pressing issues are his intolerance of frustration, low impulse control, and insolence.

We will completely miss the issues of character and maturity when our demand for acceptable behavior blinds us to the core issues of a child's heart. Many parents fail at the task of growing their child's character because they prefer to train a child who conforms to certain rules. Rules are necessary, and they must bring clear consequences when violated, but which rules are worth making? That's where we need wisdom.

A child's physical appearance is a huge, almost cosmic, parental issue. Do we make hard-and-fast rules about what a child wears to church? Do we make a titanic issue over a child's hair color (blue-and-red stripes) or style (bottom half of the head shaved, top half sporting a ponytail)? I'm not suggesting that it's best to have no rules with regard to these issues, but when is it really only a minor issue?

Wisdom requires knowing your bent versus your child's bent. If you seek to be respected in your community by exhibiting the appropriate social markers of accomplishment, intelligence, and power, then I can almost guarantee that one of your children will be bent to flaunt these same standards. At least one of your kids—and hopefully more—will challenge your perspective. If they don't, you'll know that you have established a family rule that supersedes loving the Lord your God more than anything else and loving others as much as you love yourself.[8] In majoring on a minor (your child's fashion choices or physical appearance), you've buried the major issue of loving God underneath the vestments of conformity to earthly standards for outward appearance.

Here is an alternative approach that draws from wisdom. Every child is unique, and every child must find the ways she can fit *in* the world and the manner in which she is not to be *of* the world.[9] A child who is too hesitant to buck the world's system must be called to test the boundaries of convention in order to obey God. On the other hand, a child who can't seem to conform to *any* rule must find how to be sufficiently "in" a larger world to engage it with her Christian perspective. Each child will have a bent in one of these directions: either to be "of" the world by conforming too closely to its values or to be "not of" this world and to stand completely apart from it. It is our task to affirm and then challenge the bent. If our child is either a rebel or a rule keeper, it is both good and not good. The good must be grown, and the not-good must meet the strength of parental resistance. The dilemma is that we seldom see good in being a rebel, and we fail to see ill in being a rule keeper. We must work both sides of the aisle to accomplish God's purpose in developing a tender and strong heart in a child. We must grow a child's ability to fit the world and also to resist the world.

It is not difficult to conceptualize this in the life of an elementary-school child. We want our children to do well in math, science, and English. We want them to attain high marks in sports, music, and scholastics. We want them to be popular, well-behaved, and respectful of others. This is how they are to fit in the world. However, we want our children to believe in biblical morality and values and to possess eternal convictions. We don't want them to cheat, steal, or cuss. We want them to be good Christians. In this way, they are not of this world. However, is this the only distinction between "in and not of" that ought to guide our understanding of rules?

If it is, then we are not bound to the Bible, but to a bland, religiously middle-class existence. We desire to raise a "good" child primarily so we'll have a trophy that authenticates the goodness of our family. We hesitate to go all the way in raising a daring, risk-taking young believer whose boldness reflects the wild, incomprehensible goodness of a loving and forgiving God. A family that upholds Scripture will acknowledge the inevitability of sin, separation, and sorrow in all dimensions of life and relationships as well as the wild winds of God's healing grace. Therefore it is abominable to raise a child who might one day fit the description of the prodigal's self-righteous older brother or the materialistic rich young ruler.[10] Our aspirations for our children have to far exceed the wish that they be merely "good."

Would we be pleased with our son's choice to give his life to conservation and environmentalism, to honor and care for the earth? Or would we view this child as a misguided political misfit? Would we try to steer him toward the more acceptable vocation of missionary, or would we find even this path to be too threatening? For many Christian parents, the fields of business, law, or medicine better fit the conventional notion of the "good" life.

Wisdom also calls us to recognize that our children must be "in and not of" the culture of Christendom. If they always do the acceptable thing according to the rules of the church community, we are inviting them to conform to human expectations more than to know the hard requirements of Christ. We need a better approach than merely conforming to cultural Christianity.

As we've seen, wisdom relies on listening to God and to our children. So now it's time to listen. Every child must teach her parents on the basis of her unique, God-given bent. For one child, showing up at a formal party wearing jeans would bring the death of embarrassment; for another, wearing a dress to the same party would be like walking on hot coals. Christian parenting is not demanding the opposite of whatever your child is naturally inclined to do. Instead it involves helping your child learn how to live in and then out of the box, long enough and freely enough to know what it means to hear the name she will one day be called, the new name that God will give her. Her natural bent is right now whispering that name.

Trusting God During the Tough Times

I know no greater pain than watching my children suffer. The moments when I've watched another little child push one of my kids on the playground, or when a young man has broken my daughter's heart, have frightened me with the fury that rises within. I'm a father, and it's my bent to protect my children from harm. I can bear the childish push on the playground with relative self-control, but the deeper wounds and injustices of life draw to the surface a demand that says, "Hurt me, but don't touch my child!"

I believe to the deepest recesses of my being that we must suffer if we are to mature; and that is one way that being parents grows us up. It is true for parents, and I ache that it is also true for my children. My kids will not always be chosen for the school play or asked to go to the prom, but when they are rejected and I see the brooding hurt or tear-lined face, I want to do whatever it takes to ease their pain.

A parent who doesn't feel these overwhelming sensations is either emotionally detached or, even worse, overtly hostile. If we are not willing to take a bullet for our children, then we have not allied our souls with their well-being. On the other hand, to succumb to the urge to protect without self-control and wisdom is to smother and envelop our child in the insufferable mesh of our own soul. The overly protective parent not only suffocates a child, but creates a Siamese-twin relationship that conforms the child to the parent's bent rather than allowing the child to develop along the path of God's choosing.

It is a parent's calling to model how to suffer well. Children will only come to value the redemptive power of suffering if they see it lived out in the life of their parents. Children must come to see that calamity introduces us to our limits, to our neediness, and to our weakness. Pain reminds us of our desperate need for our Father. If Jesus learned obedience through suffering, then so must my children.[11] But how long is enough? When is intervening to stop or lessen the suffering actually wisdom rather than suffocating protection? When is allowing a child to endure suffering just a false front for emotional abuse? Wisdom doesn't offer formulaic answers, nor does it take away the risk that we might well fail even when we long to do well.

One clue to knowing the right answer to "How long?" is to listen to the voices of our past. When we were the age of our children, where did we fail and suffer and wish a parent had rescued us? The answer can tell us where we are too apt to step in prematurely to protect our children. Or where did our parents overdo things to keep us from suffering? That might be the place where we are apt to let our children suffer for too long. Our parenting habits often are a reaction to what we wanted and did not receive from our own parents.

Another clue comes from listening to the bent of our child. One child may flinch at the first hint of a fearful circumstance, and another may launch himself straight into the face of imminent disaster. The key to both tendencies is the balance demanded by being "in and not of" this world. To be in this world means we know how to calculate, in light of our capacities and desires, the risks and rewards of any danger. It is likely foolish to continue in a basketball program if your son is the shortest kid in his class unless he truly loves the game and bears other marks of strength, like superb speed and agility.

What does wisdom demand? Do we let our children warm the bench in basketball when they might be fantastic long-distance runners? Do we let our son play with older boys in the neighborhood even though he is often the one who gets hurt or is left out? The real means to determine the moment of intervention is through conversation with our child. The best intervention is not unilateral, but dialogical. True dialogue requires a knowledge of our child's bent. Is he verbal or reclusive? Does he bear a low or high threshold of pain? Does he allow the words and opinions of peers to regularly influence his choices?

Knowing how a child thinks, at least in part, allows us to ask her the tough questions: "How are you going to address your verbally abusive coach? What will you do when the older kids make fun of you?" Dialogue invites the child to name what she wants from you and when she is willing to let you intervene. This is part of listening to your child so you can gain wisdom.

My daughter Amanda had a teacher who seemed to treat her with patronizing contempt. I eventually found out that Amanda had chosen not to tell me for fear I'd go to the school and make a scene. When we finally talked about it, the first portion of our dialogue took us through a few past encounters where I had made matters worse due to my anger. It was painful and humbling to hear these things from my daughter. I apologized and made it clear that my past failures would not be repeated, but neither would I ignore the sorry situation her teacher had created.

We settled on a plan. Amanda would first seek the counsel of the assistant principal. She would then talk directly to the teacher, and we role-played various scenarios. If a good resolution was not reached after she talked with the teacher, Amanda would ask the assistant principal to mediate. If this plan didn't work, then and *only* then would I get involved. Wisdom is learned in the interplay of dialogue, the humility of confession, and the planning and praying for redemption.

PLAYING IN LIFE'S PARADOX

If suffering is the soil for maturing, then redemption is the context for becoming a child again. It is in the face of the unexpected and piercing kindness of a stranger, an enemy, or God that we find ourselves laughing with delight and confusion. How can I be both strong and weak, needy and confident, self-centered and loving, and blind and able to see? It is all a grand, glorious, and awful paradox.

Wise parents know the bent of their child and also the bent of their own souls. They know what it means to help their child be in the world and not of it, therefore allowing the child to enter risk, failure, pain, and loss, but only for a season. And God uses all this to impart wisdom as they carry on the continuous dialogue with their children. It is also meant to lead both parent and child to grasp and be grasped by the poetry of paradox.

Being "in and not of," after all, is a paradox of life. Child-oriented wisdom is not a straight line to a quick answer or an easy solution, but a journey of love and growth that leads to success as God defines it, both for parents and for children.

CHAPTER 3

Know Your Child's Brave New World

Why We Need to Raise a Generation of Activists

The day had been mired in the adult struggles of ministry decisions, which meant facing the hard reality that we could not afford our dreams. If fiscal responsibility involves not presuming on the will of God, then shouldn't we determine what to do based on what we can afford? If we are carrying out God's vision, though, shouldn't we move ahead and trust the Lord to provide the funds?

The meeting was an encounter between two interdependent and contentious species, the dreamers and the managers. I waffled. I coaxed. I grumbled. I sneaked a look at my new sailing magazine. In the end we postponed our decision until we could obtain more data. Sometimes it's wiser to table a discussion and hope Jesus returns before we are forced to decide.

I was adrift between two worlds that always seem to be in conflict: desire and necessity. It happens at work and away from work. For instance, I really want to buy a new sailboat. But I have kids who need to eat regularly, wear clothes that aren't threadbare, and go to college. I might be able to buy a boat now and still send my kids to college, but it's safer to save my money and buy a boat later—to just buy some more boating magazines and forget about the boat itself. But providing food, clothes, and college tuition seems dull and dutiful; sailing seems scintillating and sensuous. It's necessity versus desire.

I felt exhausted by the decisions we refused to make at the meeting and the ache and irritation that often come from the bumper pool game of unrequited desire. My solution to those moments is to get busy. I made phone calls, answered e-mail inquiries, and eventually checked my voice mail to find two messages. The first was from my daughter Amanda saying she was leaving a school dance and would be a few minutes late picking me up at the ferry. (We live on an island.) The second was from my wife. I heard her first sentence and froze. She said, "Amanda has been arrested. She is in jail." It couldn't be true, but the pale, gray tone of my wife's voice left no doubt that it was. The day's earlier hassles disappeared. I was about to be introduced to my child's brave new world.

New World or Just a Remake?

We know our children's world is not the same as the one in which we grew up. We also know that our kids face certain realities that are quite similar to the ones every generation must address. It is both a completely new world and a profound remake of all the days that have preceded us.

Everything changes and everything remains the same. Our parents could not have conceived of checking to see if an evening next week is free by pulling out a PDA. Our children can't comprehend why their parents are unable to change the blinking 12:00 A.M. on the VCR. But the fact remains that, for *every* age, two realities of life will always be true: Children (and the rest of us) struggle both for intimacy and for autonomy. We want to be close to those we love, but we don't want to be so close that we are absorbed into another. And we want both of these at the same time.

A teenager wants the girl of his dreams, but he doesn't want her to tell him what to wear and how to act. A teenager may believe in the same God that her parents do, but she simply can't agree to everything they think and do and still be uniquely herself. Children consider it their right and privilege to be different, while parents still believe that children need not be *that* different. There is a necessary tension between intimacy and autonomy.

Intimacy brings a sense of safety: I am cared for and protected in the womb of a close relationship or tightly knit group. For generations people remained in the same community and worked in the same trade for life. Staying put brought a powerful sense of safety. The family, community, or business set the parameters of acceptability. If you work here, you will wear the company uniform. If you worship here, you will believe in inerrancy. As long as the rules are obeyed, the intimacy will last. If you disobey, though, you run the risk of exclusion and loneliness. This was paid-for intimacy and rule-based acceptance, making the sense of safety an illusion. In truth, this was neither safe nor intimate.

Autonomy is a search for uniqueness and personal meaning. Who am I? What am I to be, to do, to dream? Autonomy takes us from safety and intimacy to danger and to our unique calling in life. Intimacy may succor and shield, nurture and satisfy, but autonomy calls us to see and seek beyond the horizon of home with the aim of exploring and conquering worlds not known to us. To be an individual who is separate from others, to differentiate ourselves from those with whom we are intimate, is always to get into trouble. And trouble and tension disrupt intimacy.

Remember that our children are constantly asking us two questions. Intimacy asks, "Am I loved?" Autonomy asks, "Can I get my own way?" When the two mix, the question becomes "Will you love me even if I choose to be someone you'd prefer I not become?" These questions make every generation largely the same. Parenting well and learning to be raised by your children require that you recognize how each generation tends to approach these same questions with a different worldview.

Recycling the Generations

Historians William Strauss and Neil Howe have done us a tremendous favor in two books, *Generations* and *The Fourth Turning*. In those books they delineate a fascinating overview of the repetitive cycles of history. Beginning with the founding of the American colonies, they look at four repeating cycles, each of which lasts a generation (twenty to twenty-five years). Their copious research and elegant theory bring together something intuitively expressed by many: History repeats itself. I am profoundly influenced by the studies of Strauss and Howe, but in this chapter I will focus on a more theological and psychological interplay of generational conflict.[1]

All of us face an oscillating pattern not only in our individual lives, our families, and our societal institutions, but also in generations. The pattern arises due to our conflicted efforts to trust a God who can't be seen and can't be manipulated to accomplish our purposes. The seasons of our souls follow the four cycles of the generations: from blessing to presumption to awakening to calamity. Calamity gives rise once again to God's blessing through rescue and redemption, and the cycle then repeats itself.

Let me illustrate this pattern as found in one of the laments in the writings of the prophet Hosea:

I am the LORD your God, who rescued you from your slavery in Egypt.
You have no God but me, for there is no other savior. I took care of
you in the wilderness, in that dry and thirsty land. But when you had
eaten and were satisfied, then you became proud and forgot me. So
now I will attack you like a lion, or like a leopard that lurks along
the road. I will rip you to pieces like a bear whose cubs have been
taken away. I will tear you apart and devour you like a hungry lion.

You are about to be destroyed, O Israel, though I am your helper.
Where now is your king? Why don't you call on him for help?
Where are all the leaders of the land? You asked for them, now let

them save you! In my anger I gave you kings, and in my fury I took them away.[2]

THE ERA OF BLESSING

God blesses and rescues us from slavery because he is committed to rescuing and to redeeming. He is our Savior and our Caregiver who provides food and drink to satisfy our hungry and thirsty souls. God loves to give. He gives us a vast array of his glory through the taste of a sweet plum and the warm arms of a grandmother, and the soothing lullaby of a mother's soft voice. We are meant to be stewards of the blessing of God's gifts. A steward doesn't own the gifts. Instead, she manages them for the good of those around her. A good steward neither hoards nor wantonly gives away the goods for ill-gotten gain. She is other-focused, seeking their good.

Furthermore, a steward receives the gifts of God with gratitude and offers them humbly to God in the sacrifice of praise. A steward knows the agony of deprivation yet makes sure there is plenty for all. She will sacrifice almost everything to keep life in order. If, like me, you are a member of the Baby Boom generation, our grandparents were the stewards in the era of blessing.

The constantly asked question "Am I loved?" typifies our children's generation, but not that of our grandparents. To ask if they were loved would have seemed too selfish. And the question "Can I get my own way?" would also have been inconceivable. Their primary concern was not to dishonor their parents, family, community, or country. For our great-grandparents, raising a good steward would be no more difficult than providing food, housing, and some degree of education. Morality and method were already part of the fabric of the world. Their mode of parenting was about as straight-line as it gets.

But the era of blessing doesn't last forever. When God provides for us and we are satisfied, then we turn from him. We confuse God's blessing with earthly success, and we attribute it to our own cleverness and skill. We become confident builders of a new world that will have less pain and more pleasure, less need for trust and more autonomy to do as we wish. This is when the era of blessing turns into the era of presumption.

THE ERA OF PRESUMPTION

If blessing characterized our grandparents' generation, then presumption took over in our parents' era. But why presumption? Our desire for God is muted when the life he provides—the gifts from his hand—become more desirable to us than the Gift-Giver himself. A life of ease gives us time to rest and play, and soon we forget our earlier hunger. We presume that we *deserve* his gifts, and over time we forget God. Pride not only presumes that we deserve what we have, but it compels us to demand even more. It is during this period of high confidence that people turn to using the gifts preserved by the stewards (their parents) to build the cities of man. The generation of the era of presumption wants to build a human kingdom that will solve every problem confronting humankind.

The builders (again, our parents' generation, if you're a Baby Boomer) adopted a utilitarian approach to life. They took the stories and symbols of the stewards and turned them into a pragmatic, streetwise economy. A builder is less concerned with why and more interested in what. A builder becomes a survivor who knows how to capitalize on the moment and get the best of what is available. He believes in morality and the stories of redemption, but he would rather make new stories than remember what his steward parents preserved from the era of blessing.

The core question of our children—"Am I loved?"—still was not a viable question even for the builders. They assumed the answer was "Of course!" Likewise, the answer to "Can I get my own way?" was also assumed to be "Of course!" You can create your own success in the military, through education, or in business. You can choose to live in the suburbs and join the right clubs. All you need is the moxie and native intelligence to do so. When our fathers returned from World War II, they felt empowered to deny the past and get on with the future. Indeed, they *could* get their own way.

The era of presumption maintained the builders' primary goal of keeping their children out of the wrong crowd and making steady progress toward their own success. Builders kept their vision sufficiently optimistic to avoid the nightmarish memories of Pearl Harbor, Dachau, and Hiroshima. It was time to build a new future, not grieve the past. So we got Campus Crusade for Christ and Disneyland, the rebuilding of Europe, and America's vast, endless suburbs of hope.

But there is a dark side to a time of optimism and its presumption that we can accomplish *anything* if we just put our mind to it. The dark side is self-righteousness and greater division between the haves and the have-nots. It's a time where hubris is masked as the guise of being a good parent, or citizen, or Christian; but self-centeredness is left unchallenged as long as a person plays by the well-recognized rules of the culture. Self-righteousness, however, always migrates south to the rotting of society's foundation and to the perversion of values and morality. Remember, this was the generation of the Kennedys and Richard Nixon, leaders who set new standards both for amazing public achievements and incredible personal failure. The era of presumption—no matter what century—is eventually disrupted by a period of awakening. Since the children of the builders came of age in an era of awakening, the can-do builders found parenting to be uniquely chaotic as they tried to raise their Boomer kids.

THE ERA OF AWAKENING

It is inevitable that, in the midst of a self-satisfied and self-idolizing society, someone will note that the age is fat and full of itself. There is always a significant minority that is not allowed to enjoy the prosperity of the age. So a prophetic movement begins that exposes the era as being complacent and foolish. Voices arise to reveal the danger that looms if the society of presumption refuses to repent and change. More often than not, the prophet is shunned, shamed, and even killed rather than heeded. We need look no further into the past than Dr. Martin Luther King Jr. and many other lesser-known martyrs from the civil rights movement.

The prophet does begin to find a following, however, by creating a new vision for society. He stands outside the mainstream as both a compelling and a contemptuous figure. He intrigues and offends; therefore he destabilizes the status quo. He exposes the soft underbelly of comfort and ease that was created by the can-do builders. The prophet is a dreamer. He is more inward, subjective, and idealistic than his builder parents.

If you are a Boomer, this is a description of your generation, the era of awakening. Many of us were marching against the war or in support of civil rights, doing drugs and promoting free love, or believing that Jesus was returning soon because the signs pointed to this being not only the Age of Aquarius, but also the coming of God's kingdom. The gospel was going to extend to every person, language, and nation in our lifetime. Why *our* lifetime and not someone else's? Only because we insisted on getting our own way, and we were convinced that we were loved. We were so loved, in fact, that the world revolved around us.

Ah, the heady days of youth. Do we really know that we are deeply and passionately loved? Not at all. But it's true that more of life is now revolving around the whims of a single generation—the Boomers—than at any time in history. We have parents who were guided by Dr. Benjamin Spock. Our self-image and self-esteem are as important to us as our performance and our standing in relationship with others. We have become a jumble of ironies. We are unique, but in a herd. We rebel together. We convert to Christ together. We are more autonomous than any other generation, but the price is a higher need for intimacy and connectedness.

The era of awakening careens eventually toward intermittent crisis and then to a time of calamity that redefines the nature of life. It is the children of the Boomers who will take all that has come before and face this present challenge.

THE ERA OF CALAMITY

A transitional period between awakening and the coming calamity is marked by indulgence, cynicism, faultfinding, and mockery. So far I'm only describing the ethos of irony popularized by Jay Leno and David Letterman. And here is the tragedy: I love both of their shows. I suppose they are the cynical prophets we deserve. They mock everyone, including themselves. They are the court jesters who tweak the noses of Billy Graham and Bill Clinton with equal ardor. They expose our foibles and help focus us on our flawed humanity. But they come up empty when it comes to building anything.

The era of awakening—the Boomer generation—opened the door to idealist hope that eventually got trampled when the revolutionaries of the sixties took to selling insurance and mutual funds. Indeed, during the Reagan eighties the Boomers lost their change-the-world religion. And what or who will take its place? Leno and Letterman remind us nightly that we have lost our moorings, so we might as well hear about a Hollywood celebrity's current flirtations and vapid opinions. Who cares? Really, who cares? The sad answer: We all do. We have nothing better to care about because we've lost hope that anything can ever really change.

And here is the insanity. Many parents say they want to protect their children from the horrors of the sex, drugs, and rock and roll of this receding and decadent era, and yet they show far more concern for their stock portfolios, their standing at church, and their waistline than the matters of hunger, AIDS, bigotry, sexism, white-collar crime, and the growing hatred and violence in homes, families, churches, and society. We are in an age not only of inanity but also insanity.

Let us name this current age well. We are not stewards or builders or even the prophets and dreamers of the sixties and seventies. Fat and indulgent, we have careened through the trickle-down eighties into the raging, financially prosperous nineties, and then stumbled into the post-9/11 bust. Fat 401(k) plans were gutted by a combination of the downturn in the market, the avarice of corporate CEOs, and the greed of overconfidence. It is a new but not so glamorous day.

On the other side of the world, and perhaps as close as next door, a radical extremist is building a bomb or plotting an intricate scheme to wreak devastation on the United States or its perceived allies. The Middle East, always a land of bitter hatred and violence, at any time could boil over again and light the entire kitchen on fire, with the rest of the house threatened by the growing flames.

Back home in America, we litigate everything, and we trust no one, especially a leader. If a person wants to lead, she will be decimated by the news media and her peers. The smallest matter of a person's life is available for public scrutiny and biased debate. Our favorite sport is impaling a person on innuendo and gossip. I'm no longer describing a cynic such as Leno or Letterman, but our colleagues in the company lunchroom, the foyer at church, and the family room of our homes. We live in a meanspirited, brutal, and divisive era. This is the era that we Boomers have delivered to our children. And it is in this era that we need to redefine the high calling of parenting.

The aftermath of presumption and pride is always a hard fall. (Remember the words of Hosea.) The fall can be self-generated, such as the onset of heart disease for those who indulge in too much rich food and too little exercise. Or it can be caused by others, as is the case for those who have been locked out of the benefits of the age. The poor rise up. The slaves rebel. Or, in the case of those Hosea begged to wake up, God rose up and brought harm to them as a wild beast tears at its prey. It is in this era that we need a generation of ordinary leaders who prize the passion and heart of God and who, with God's provision, will heroically rise to face the calamity.

Our children are growing up in this era of calamity. We need to prepare them for reality, for the calamities to come. We need to raise a generation of leaders, a generation of God-loving activists.

An activist is often an unimposing force who seems to be called out of anonymity to excel at a task that seems greater than anyone can face. In his humility he finds the boldness to do what few are willing to risk. He has the pragmatism of his grandparents and the skepticism of his parents. He is skilled in the ways of the world and is cynical and world-weary, but he craves something new that is worth living and dying to achieve. If you're a Boomer, your son or daughter needs to become this activist.

Hope on the Horizon

There is a remarkable consistency to the four cycles of generations, arising from the cycle of sin and redemption that inevitably leads to the sequential cycles of blessing, presumption, awakening, and calamity. Cultures and generations rise out of the ashes of our inexorable struggle with God and our inevitable struggle with the tension between intimacy and autonomy. These struggles will continue as long as we reside in a fallen world. As dark as the moment may seem—and ours is a day with storm clouds swirling—it is not a day where Leno and Letterman will have the final, cynical word.

What is unique about our children's generation that holds out hope for their rising up to meet the coming calamity? I will suggest three fundamental areas, each one revolving around colliding contradictions and the intensity of life's paradox. In each of these areas, God calls parents to confront the growing complexity of today's world.

GLUT AND DEPRIVATION

Today we see more, hear more, and feel more than any other generation in history. Our technology mimics God's omnipresence. I can see the flaming ruins of warfare in the West Bank and then switch channels to watch a medical team insert a camera into the end of a microscopic probe and an in-utero child put his fingers in his mouth. In another operation, however, a child the same age is considered tissue and is killed with saline and extricated with forceps. Which is it: prized child or organic debris? In this era of calamity, it's a matter of semantics and a question of who controls the use of language.

Words flock around us like pigeons and litter us with their detritus. There are too many signs, symbols, advertisements, sound bites, and slogans to bear hearing or seeing anything that is not radically stimulating and intriguing. We are deprived of the ability to choose, dissect, and critique, so we often go broke and hungry in a world of utter prodigality. I have watched my son endlessly search for the right Web site to get the exact information he needs for a school paper. He knows it's there, so he just has to keep looking. By the time he gets some of what he was looking for, he has little energy or time left to write the research paper. He's a victim of too much data.

This glut has taken us to the edge of futility and isolation. Any effort to achieve omnipresence will leave us little space or time to call our own. If we are everywhere, we are nowhere. It would be wonderful if we could actually think globally and act locally. Instead we remain inert as we gather more information and do more thinking, all the while becoming deadened to the world around us. We simply know too much, and it paralyzes us.

What then happens with our parenting? We have received too much input, too many influences, too much pressure. So we wear our kids out dragging them everywhere so they can do everything. We drive them from music lessons to soccer practice to youth group meetings to exhaustion. They live in the car and long for sleep. By insisting that they do everything, we are not preparing our children for action; we are inuring them by stress and pressure. And this is exactly the opposite of what we should be doing. The era of calamity calls for a generation of activists. And it's up to us to train them.

SUSPICION AND GULLIBILITY

We are gullible enough to believe almost anything, but we are trusting less and less. We believe in the latest fad diet, the magical power of a new car to make us more glamorous, and that extraterrestrials have been visiting our planet. Or maybe not. Aren't UFOs just a hoax perpetrated by the Soviet Union, the evil empire? Oh no, that empire dissolved years ago. Russia is now a friend, and we have a new enemy: Iraq. Or has that changed again? The target seems to keep moving.

We trust no one except our friends, but even the closest ally can become an enemy when circumstances change. Good guys are also bad guys, and vice versa. We hate this ethical grayness, so we choose instead to see things in black and white. For instance, Israel is good because the Jews were a persecuted people and because the Israeli government remains loyal to the United States. Palestinians are terrorists because they oppose Israel and kill innocent civilians. However, talk to someone on the West Bank, and you'll find that one man's terrorist is another man's freedom fighter.

People of goodwill can hold opposing views on matters of international politics. We believe we're right until circumstances change, and a new right comes along. The United States claimed the Soviet Union as an ally as long as the Soviets were waging war against Nazi Germany. After the war, however, when the Soviet Union imposed its domination over Eastern Europe, we reversed our definitions of friend and enemy.

The world is complex and full of paradox, and parenting is not exempt. Our discomfort with paradox, like the ethical grayness of bad-guy allies, causes us to look for simple solutions. We want to accept things as being either all good or all bad, and this tendency shapes the way we raise our children. The more we believe our side is right and good, the more critical we become of those who disagree with us. So when values and a worldview are taught in the home, the approach is often narrow, dogmatic, and judgmental rather than open, curious, and dialogical. Because we bristle at the complexities of life, we tend to indoctrinate our children in our own tribe's stance and vilify everyone else. This is the gullibility of believing in the complete rightness of our position, paired with the suspicious distrust of any view that differs from ours. But falling back on the black-and-white simplicity of prefab convictions inevitably feeds both suspicion and gullibility. It actually takes us farther and delivers us to the doorstep of self-righteousness.

SELF-RIGHTEOUSNESS AND SELF-DOUBT

We have access to way too much information about too many things. The Internet and cable news programs tempt us to think we could someday know everything. But omniscience belongs only to God. And as we have seen, as soon as I'm convinced that I'm right, a new right comes along and takes its place.

Our world is far too complex to figure out. But it's nothing compared to the challenge of raising children. Our children are growing up in an era of calamity, and they are constantly asking, "Am I loved?" and "Can I get my own way?" In answering their two core questions, we wade into incredible complexity. Kids need to know that they are loved and that they can't get their own way, but they need to know these facts in the context of their own era.

This need brings us to the paired reality of self-righteousness and self-doubt. Each of us has a natural bent in one of two directions. We either feel more comfortable with God's mercy ("You are loved") or with his strength ("You can't get your own way"). It's easy to assume that the way we are wired is the *right* way. Self-righteousness tempts us to elevate one above the other, asserting that the real solution is to exert more strength—or dispense more mercy—depending on our natural bent. The paradox of parenting is that God calls us to reflect *both* his mercy and his strength in equal measure. We need the humility to admit that our natural tendency is only half the answer. Parenting well requires both mercy and strength, which means we are called to do much that does not come easily.

As we face what we lack, we confront self-doubt. We see that we are woefully deficient and nowhere near equal to the task of raising children. But self-doubt can humble us so that we are ready for God to make us complete in the midst of paradox. Love and discipline, intimacy and autonomy—our kids need all of these in equal measure. And thus we have the necessary paradoxes of parenting well.

The Beginning of the Story

You may remember that I received a troubling voice-mail message from my wife. I caught the ferry that day knowing I was headed not home, but to the police station. My daughter had been arrested, I didn't know for what. I only knew that I was totally exhausted. I had spent a number of hours earlier that day caught up in the utter importance of my world, wrestling with incomprehensible difficulties that had to be surmounted, and I wanted both then and now to escape. I wanted to step onto a forty-foot sailboat in the British Virgin Islands, never answer another phone call or e-mail, and never be required to make another decision. Life was just too complex.

As I walked the three hundred yards from the ferry terminal to the police station, I asked God for help. And he spoke to me, not in an audible voice and not with a dramatic sign, but he spoke. He said, "Will you offer your daughter mercy, or will you offer judgment? What will it be, Dan, my tenderness or your anger?"

Children invite their parents to enter a brave new world, a complex world of difficulty and paradox, the era of calamity. Will we accept their invitation?

CHAPTER 4

Discerning the Voices of Our Parents

Breaking Free from the Past to Raise Our Children Well

I f you're reading the chapters of this book in sequence, you know that I had to go from my office to the police station to check on my daughter. My children aren't the type to get into trouble with the law, and I had no idea what awaited me there. The last time I'd been in a similar situation, I was my daughter's age. I was sitting in a jail cell waiting for my parents to arrive. I had left my girlfriend's house after drinking some of her father's Scotch. I had hopped in my car to drive home, and I remember feeling the rush of air on my arms as I slid around corners. I saw the flashing red lights in my rearview mirror, and without a moment's hesitation I stepped on the gas. The joyride ended with me spinning my car onto someone's lawn to avoid crashing into a police barricade.

The rush of lights, the stern faces, and the barked command to step out of the car with my hands in the air came as a terrible wake-up call. I don't remember much else. I do recall sitting in a jail cell, imagining my mother's face when she came with my father to claim her son. I dreaded her tears. I knew that she'd be crying and that my father would be silent.

I returned from this disturbing memory to the present just as I was crossing the police station parking lot. My wife had arrived already; tears and quiet fury pulled at her eyes. In the moments to come I would be asked to address my wife, my daughter, and my mother. All were present, even though my mother was actually more than two thousand miles away.

I was there to claim my daughter, but all I could hear was the hurt and disappointed voice of my mother. The voices of our children are often drowned out by other voices that shout without making a sound. And one of the loudest is the lingering influence of our parents.[1]

The Shout of Silence

John and Marty were young parents with two sweet girls, ages five and three. The girls loved to explore and play together. The older daughter, Kim, was the little caregiver and the watchful eyes of her mother. Jamey was a precocious live wire who loved to bumble into trouble and then see how her big sister would rescue her. It was a lovely duet—care and trouble meeting to give each other playful meaning.

Or at least that's how John and Marty saw the girls. But John's parents took a different view. They were all for children as long as they were off at school or away at a playground. But a home was a different matter. It was for serious living and not play. When the grandparents visited, the tension in John and Marty's home rose, and the fun declined. John became more authoritarian and began interrupting the drama of the little girls' play. The more he intruded, the more Marty felt obliged to protect the girls, and a cool distance grew between the two.

Like little weather vanes, the girls knew instinctively which way the wind was blowing. Kim became more patronizing while Jamey grew more irascible. The tension grew until calamity occurred: Jamey was overly energetic at the dinner table, pushing her place setting and sending it clattering to the floor. This opened a valve that vented all the pent-up pressure. The grandparents now had indisputable proof that John and Marty were complete failures as parents. John now had an unfathomable load of shame to carry around. And Marty had to bite her tongue to keep from challenging the withering glare of John's disapproving parents. The family was collapsing under the weight of the deafening, unspoken voices that had invaded the home.

We're foolish if we fail to see that our parents' voices keep us from hearing our children. If we are ever to learn to listen to our children, we must first recognize the influence of our parents' voices—either for ill or for good.

Why Aren't Parents Grandparents?

Fortunately, John's disapproving parents are not the norm in most extended families. There are countless times I've heard a parent say, "I only wish my dad had fathered me the way I see him relate to my son." It is both a tragedy and a glory. How could a father fail to play with his son but spend hours playing with his grandson? Is it the issue of having more free time after retirement? Are we to suspect that the progress of time and the advancing reality of mortality sizably change a grandparent to be more human, generous, kind, and patient? I suspect the answer is a cautious yes to both questions, and there is another huge factor: *Grandparents are not responsible for the product.* They can leave the dilemmas of discipline and rules to the parents as they delight in the uninhibited antics and beautiful face of their grandchild.

My own grandmother was a gem. She had suffered from debilitating rheumatoid arthritis since the age of forty-five, but she still cavorted about with the impishness of a gnome. She came to live with our family just as full and heady adolescence overcame me. There were many pitched family battles that she hobbled into with her broken body and beautiful smile. She would look at the combatants with a knowing eye and then say, "What is all this fussing about? Don't you know a boy has to goad his parents or he won't have a mind of his own?"

She became a trusted interpreter who helped me decipher the meaning of my mother's words. No doubt she also helped my mother make sense of my teenage gibberish. My grandmother kept dialogue alive between two warring sides who couldn't trust each other, but who equally trusted the one who loved us both.

It is a trustworthy adage with only a few exceptions: Grandparents and their grandkids do better with each other than parents do with either their own parents or their children. But why? Often the answer is a simple truism. Grandparents are there to spoil their grandkids, get them jazzed on sugar, and then drop them off at Mom and Dad's when the kids are about to hit the wall. There is truth to that sentiment, but far more can be said.

Grandparents are not called to provide the same day-to-day discipline and care that is the responsibility of a parent. They are meant to impart the wisdom that comes from their stance of unconditional love. A grandparent shines delight on a young face, delight that is not altered by a child's poor grades or lack of obedience. In the warm aura of such delight, wisdom can be imparted that, when offered by a parent, friend, or coach, would be scoffed at or ignored, but coming from a grandparent will be cherished for a lifetime. Every child needs this type of grandparent.

Parents might grow jealous of a grandparent's privileged status, but they should rejoice that there is a loving adult who can play that vaunted role in a child's life. More tragic is when a grandparent lives too far away to offer that care, or when a grandparent fails to see the need to be both infinitely kind and wise for his or her grandchildren. No matter what the role of the grandparent, a parent will still be called to a more demanding role and one that is likely to be played out in reaction to one's parents. It is crucial that we hear the noise that comes from the complex interplay of raising our children under the invisible but very real scrutiny of our own parents.

Hearing Our Parents' Voices

The acorn never falls too far from the oak. For all our efforts to learn from our parents' mistakes and offer the next generation a better world, we often not only repeat the same mistakes, but we add to the mix our own failed attempts to parent well. We raise our children similarly to the way we were raised—with a twist. The twist is that, in some form, we reverse the pattern in a way that shouts, "I am *not* my mother (or father)." We selectively reverse our approach in the areas where we believe our parents' methods harmed or hampered us.

My parents enjoyed the blessings of postwar prosperity that came because my father and many others shouldered the burden of fighting World War II. They were the glorious victors of war who in their child-rearing years became protectors of the stories and myths of the day.

I was born in 1952 and came of age with Jimi Hendrix, Led Zeppelin, and the Beatles. I am narcissistic enough to believe that hard rock—and even acid rock—was far less damaging to my psyche than those who suffered the onslaught of Elvis or his resurgence in disco. But that is how a Boomer born in the early fifties thinks—inward, pessimistic, judgmental, and oh so proud.

My family was ill prepared for the turbulent years of the sixties. My father was a blue-collar worker without a college education living in an uppity, middle-class suburb that served as a bedroom community for a state university. My father was uncomfortable in that milieu, so he withdrew. My mother stood in the gap and plunged into all the socially approved clubs and meetings.

My parents allowed me to set the parameters of my friendships and activities. They didn't compel me to get good grades and seldom worried about whether I was well adjusted or happy. They lived their lives and I lived mine, nearby but not too close. In that sense I lived in a typical home with builder parents who allowed their children to be free. But the price is a high level of self-absorption or self-indulgence on the part of the child. I didn't face real consequences for my actions, but I knew that I was very important to the life of my family. In other words, I was loved, and I could get my own way.

A dear friend grew up in a home quite different from mine. His parents enforced rigid, authoritarian rules. They required my friend to keep his hair cut short and to attend ROTC meetings during college—and that in the social upheaval of the antiwar sixties. On the other hand, they were aloof and emotionally unavailable. Their home was authoritarian but distant. He was not loved, and he could not get his own way.

My friend obeyed the rules and deeply wanted to find someone who would care for him. His stable and warm demeanor eventually brought him into relationship with a young woman. They were married for twenty-three years, but the marriage eventually ended because she was tired of his unvarying consistency and his unwillingness to play or take a risk. He had to deal with the fallout of his parents' answers to his two core questions.

In my parents' awkwardness with facing the storms of the sixties, they assured me that, yes, I was loved. And yes, I could get my own way. These answers left me craving order, but being highly suspicious of anyone who tried to control me. My friend's parents made it clear that, no, he was not loved. And no, he could not get his own way. Faced with a lack of love and too much control, he became reserved and lonely, but conservative and well ordered until years later when his facade cracked and his marriage ended.

What kind of family did you grow up in? Did you know for certain that you were loved? Did you sense that your parents loved you enough to keep you from getting your own way? We have to know how our parents answered the two core questions for us during our childhood before we can understand our own inclination in answering the two questions for our children.

Children will stand against their parents even when the children become parents themselves. We react to our parents' approach to life, and that enables us to set a new course and engage the unique issues of our day with greater freedom. On the other hand, each of us perpetuates some of what our parents built into us, whether good or ill.

My parents seldom questioned me about my grades or vocational dreams. On the other hand, they insisted that I be involved in a number of social groups (Boy Scouts, Masons, football), which served as the context for shaping my morality and character. Now, as a father, I often do just the opposite. I obsess over my kids' grades and seldom ever view a social organization (including the church youth group) as a primary place for my children to mature. On the other hand, I have frightened myself by points of similarity with my own parents. Fights with my children over issues of dress and hairstyle and body piercing coincide with the wars my parents and I fought over my rebellious teenage appearance.

Reaction and replication are normal and necessary. However, they are not the same as being creative. We need to create something entirely new from the raw materials our parents gave us. Our children live in a different world, and we have to listen to *their* voice if we are to learn how to parent them well.

Responding to Our Parents' Voices

There are countless ways we can respond to the voices, the pressure, and the presence of our parents. But the four most common ways are proving, seeking approval, fixing, or paying back. Each has its benefits and its clear disadvantages.

PROVING THAT FATHER KNOWS BEST

Jane loved her father fiercely. There is a picture of the two of them standing on a ridge in the Greenbrier Mountains staring out into the dusky evening, both wearing khakis, starched white shirts, and sailor caps. Her father would always look at the picture and say, "Chip off the old block." Jane's siblings knew that they were loved, but no one doubted that Jane was their dad's favorite.

The family was sophisticated and urbane. The children were to be well dressed, well mannered, and, depending on the moment, cynical and above the rules that governed life's commoners. Jane's parents allowed the children to be rebellious when it fit the family's reputation. For instance, the kids were allowed to sample wine and cocktails at a young age. When Jane and her siblings became teenagers, the parents didn't object if they drank too much—as long as none of them was driving. The rules of Jane's family were, "Yes, you are loved (or at least indulged)," and "Yes, you can get your own way (as long as you don't shame us or harm yourself)."

Jane married a cultured, well-bred man. He was considerably weaker than her father and didn't stand in her way as she bound their children to the life of her parents. Years into the marriage, Jane had a religious experience that brought her to trust Jesus as her Savior. A huge shift occurred in her life, her marriage, and, at least from an external standpoint, her parenting.

Her children were no longer allowed to participate in the drinking that was part of her parents' family feasts, and she no longer tolerated foul language. Further, she took a strong stance against any attitude of disdain toward those in a lower economic class, and she introduced a new level of discipline and care. But what did not change was Jane's fundamental loyalty to her parents' way of living.

Jane wanted her parents to know God, and she offered them books and tapes that might stir their spiritual interest. But she couldn't stand her ground and challenge the *heart* issues related to their lives. She corrected her children's behavior, but she could not name how she had been used by her father as a deeper source of emotional intimacy than his wife. His choice of Jane as his favorite had alienated his other children and set up a tragic jealousy between mother and daughter. Her family was rife with heartache, but Jane couldn't face the damage that had come as a result of her being her dad's favorite. Consequently, she was unable to see how she had bonded with her middle son and was more critical and distant with the oldest child, her daughter. She had changed the outward adornment of her parenting, but she never faced that she was replicating her dad's pattern of favoritism.

More often than not, people will replicate the structure, tone, and direction of their parents' style to the degree that the harm done by their parents is never acknowledged. There is the feeling that to name the harm might mean the loss of a privileged place in the parents' life. When people set out, either deliberately or unconsciously, to prove the goodness of their own parents, the children in the next generation can't escape the pattern established by their grandparents. But the pattern must be broken if the youngest generation is to become autonomous and free.

SERIOUSLY SEEKING APPROVAL

Earlier in this chapter I told the story of John and his two precious daughters. John's wife, Marty, grew up in a relaxed family atmosphere. John grew up in a home that approached children as if they were little soldiers who needed a lot of discipline and who ought to know they were valued without being told.

John married Marty in part because she was so different from his mother, who was regal, ordered, and precise. In stark contrast, if Marty stumbled over a pile of shoes, toys, or books in the middle of the floor, it was time to move the pile, not whip everyone into a frenzy of housecleaning. There were tensions between them, but John and Marty loved each other and adored their girls—until John's mom and dad visited. Then the house had to be cleaned, the girls put in appropriately feminine clothes, and the skin of the marriage stretched to cover up all the easy family habits that would surely cause the grandparents great discomfort.

John was running at a brisk sprint to gain his parents' blessing. In fact, he was desperate to receive the blessing he had never experienced as a child. This most often happens in a home where the answer to the question "Am I loved?" is "Didn't we provide for you and go to all your ball games and concerts? How dare you ask such a question!" It is a home where parenting is not a privilege; it is a duty, the right thing to do. This home is a world of hard work, with rewards for success and punishment for failure. This scenario is played out in the majority of the homes of those who make up conservative religious groups and political parties. It is a world governed by dogmatic either-or, us-and-them thinking. This, by the way, is not a model Christian home.

The home John grew up in had everyone starving for passion, delight, and joy, but no one could admit it. To admit being lonely, hurt, and confused would be disloyal. Most of the children in such a home can't wait until they become parents so they can do things *right*. Sadly, they don't want to do things right in order to bless their children, but in order to receive the life-giving yes that their parents have withheld.

FURIOUSLY FIXING THE MESS

It's easy to understand the popularity of self-help books. People are on a mad dash to make things better. Look at a friend's nightstand, or your own, and you'll see proof of our burning desire to become thinner, smarter, more prayerful, and less anxious. This obsession with self-improvement carries over to our parenting. We're sure that we're missing the boat when it comes to raising flawless, culturally protected, deeply spiritual, gifted children. Promising a quick fix to those who are dying to be fixed is a multimillion dollar industry.

It can, however, be overwhelming to receive all this help. That's why we now have a subgenre of self-help that gives us permission to take a break from trying to change. We can now feel less guilty about *not* working so hard to change.[2] It proves that we're exhausted from trying so hard to fix our lives.

My wife and I receive a large number of family Christmas letters. The year we received two hundred such letters, I was feeling moderately perverse as I divided the photos of smiling families into two piles on the basis of whether or not the family was wearing natty, coordinated outfits. To be fair I included our own Christmas portrait in the sorting process.

Approximately half of the families represented were involved in full-time Christian ministry. The other half were either not church oriented, or they were people of faith with careers outside the religious realm. As I sorted the photos, I found that seventy percent of the well-coordinated wardrobes came from the ranks of the professionally spiritual. Only 40 percent of the families involved in nonreligious careers were dolled up in uniform fashion. In fact, a full 15 percent of these didn't even send a picture because, as one letter stated,

"We tried, but the dog threw up during the ordeal, and we all decided we were too much a mess to worry you with our picture." I laughed until I cried. But then I scanned again the lovely, smiling faces of the many families that looked so very good.

When I took a second look at the coordinated-clothing families, my natural inclination was to try to figure out how they came to be so happy. I wanted an answer so that I could stop doing what I was doing and start doing whatever *they'd* been doing. "Next year," I wanted to promise myself, "we'll achieve this same state of nirvana so we can send out a cheery, fully coordinated family Christmas portrait." To be honest, the Allender family portrait that year was marked by us all wearing red sweaters. And everyone, including the dog, looked far happier than we were just before and immediately after the photo session.

No wonder the fix-it mentality breeds so much pressure and ultimately leads to despair. It makes us wonder why, when *everyone else* has it all figured out, we still can't get our act together. The weariness that comes from trying to fix ourselves and our kids leads to less joy and sometimes even more failure. The things we try to fix can leave the past unresolved and thus create new problems for the future.

Payback Parenting

The last of the most common responses to the noise of our parents is to shout louder than they speak. It is an effort to drown out the harm of the past by swearing we will *never* repeat it and then blaming those who raised us for the harm we suffer today. This is a most difficult issue to nuance. After all, some parents have been truly evil. Certainly a home where the core questions are answered, "No, you are not loved" and "Yes, you can get your own way because I don't care what happens to you" is a dark and destructive home.

Some homes and families are even worse than that. For many children, sexual abuse is habitual, and no one steps in to stop the harm. Physical and emotional abuse commonly go unchecked. There are homes where children are tortured or sold for pornographic purposes also without anyone to protect them. There are far more of these kinds of homes than any of us wish to imagine. Those who survive such torment find it inconceivable to think about victimizing their own children as they were victimized.

The dilemma is that a passionate desire to create a radically different home and family can often be fueled by hatred and not love. It is natural to hate what has brought us terrible harm. The problem is that hatred begets more hatred. To the degree we that we forcefully swear we will never be like our mother or father, we are almost cosmically destined to be far more like them than not. Hatred shapes us into the very thing we hate. Likewise, but far better, love shapes us into who and what we love.

Many who have suffered great harm at the hands of their parents are destined to repeat it to the degree that their fury is driving them. I worked with a woman who hated her mother, a meddlesome, untrustworthy, and defensive parent. When my client was a child, if she voiced any disappointment or disagreed with anything her mother said, she would hear, "You don't have to treat me like a slave. I'm only trying to help. If you don't want my help, I'll just leave you alone, and I'll go rot in hell."

My client hated her mother, but she could never admit her fury. Instead she put her nose to the grindstone and worked a hundred times harder not to treat her daughter with disdain and to avoid manipulating any of her decisions. My client's daughter grew to want more from her and asked countless times for her opinion. But my client refused to either give advice or to criticize, and she went overboard in expressing how proud she was of her daughter. The girl became furious. She wanted her mother to fight with her, argue with her, and be a mom, not a self-esteem-producing cheerleader.

It was Martin Luther who reputedly said, "The Christian life is like a drunk trying to get on a horse. He mounts on one side and falls off on the other. He rises and mounts on that side and falls off on the side he began." If Luther didn't say this, he should have because it's sadly and comically true. The more we aspire in anger not to be what we despise, the more we fail on the other extreme. And in many cases, no matter how determined we are, we are closer than we imagine to perpetuating the very thing we despise.

It is time to rise above the noise of our parents' voices. We need to settle on an approach in which we neither defend our parents nor prove them to be absolutely wrong. We must be able to engage our children without feeling pressured to repair our past. We must honor our parents but choose the path of parenting that we are called to follow. We must quiet our parents' voices so that we can hear clearly our children's questions, accusations, and invitations.

The wisdom we need comes through quieting the outside noise so we can listen to our children as they grow us up.

CHAPTER 5

Turning Down the Voice of Our Culture

We're Not Here to Prove That Our Children Are Great

My daughter Amanda came down the stairs just as I bellowed for the third time that everyone needed to get into the car for church. We usually run late, and today there was enough tension to make going to church seem both ridiculous and absolutely necessary. When I saw what my daughter was wearing, though, I froze. She had put on a snug pullover with spaghetti straps. In other circumstances I might not have objected, but she was *not* going to wear that to church.

I told her to run upstairs and put on another shirt. We had a moment of tension—"What's wrong with this top? It isn't revealing…" A furious father pointed Amanda to her room, and she stomped up the stairs, changed to a different outfit, and we trudged off to church.

We attend a church where it is not uncommon for people to wear sandals, shorts, jeans, and T-shirts. I've never seen our pastor in a tie. The children of parents I respect have come to church in clothes that gave me a twinge of discomfort, but also the feeling that I shouldn't be so married to man-made conventions. But when my own daughter wore a top that took me over the edge, there was no discussion or compromise. I insisted that she change, and that was that.

And why was I so unyielding? It's because of the people we identify simply as "they." What would "they" think? Of course, when I objected to Amanda's outfit, I clothed my shame in a spiritual covering: "I don't think that top is honoring to the Lord." I remember looking at my slightly tattered jeans and realizing that my mother would have a fit if she could see what I was wearing. Too much cultural noise and too little time forced my daughter and me to live with my decision. But if I want to learn to listen to the voice of my child, let alone the voice of God, I must recognize how other voices are competing for my attention.

Four cultural voices compete with one another as they send me messages about my children. These ubiquitous voices of the media, our friends, school, and the church overlap and often contradict one another. These are the voices that often prevent us from hearing our kids.

Media: Turning Down the Voice of Control

Taken together in their many forms, the media make up a sort of cultural godhead. Consider visual media such as television, movies, and video; aural media like radio, MP3s, and CDs; and print media such as newspapers, magazines, and books. Perhaps the most comprehensive medium that combines images, sound, and words is the World Wide Web. The media, considered as a conglomerate, bear the attributes of God in that they are everywhere (omnipresence), inform us about everything (omniscience), and seemingly can accomplish anything (omnipotence).

The entities that control the media control the earth. Just as the victor writes history, the media determine who is the victor. This is true in terms of who gets published, who records a CD, who is elected president, and likely which colors will be considered the hippest for fall or spring fashions. To understand the hold the media have over us, let's consider how they mirror the character of God.

OMNIPRESENCE

At almost any time, it is possible to find out what is happening in any other part of the world. The Internet enables you to converse with anyone, anywhere, at any time, no matter how disconnected you are from the real world. All that you need is the technology and the right Web address, and in a second you can sit at your desk but read an account of political unrest on the other side of the globe. Or even before the nightly news announces it, you can learn details of a bill that passed the Senate and that will immediately affect stock prices in a particular sector.

The information doesn't stop there. Some of the cheapest "entertainment" shows on television are quasi-news programs such as *60 Minutes* and *48 Hours*. With low production costs and high viewer ratings, these shows can venture far and wide to let us see into arenas that were off limits to every other generation. Furthermore, the ubiquity of news and the proliferation of technology have made it possible to simultaneously watch several news programs and seem to be everywhere important at the same moment.

The result for many people is similar to jet lag. Our bodies (space) have not caught up with the speed (time) we have been traveling; therefore we have exceeded the limits of our finiteness. The result is exhaustion. Since we can be so many places at the same time, the only normal way to function is to develop the symptoms of Attention Deficit Disorder. We can't focus on one thing because we're concentrating on everything.

Most of us are running ever faster while feeling like we're simply chasing our tails. The media invite us to expand our horizon until there is no thought of an end, a limit, or a moment to let down. As long as the ubiquity of opportunity is without a horizon, we will scramble for the thrill of omnipresence. The great tragedy is that, while we are everywhere, we are seldom with our children.

OMNISCIENCE

If we can be everywhere, then we also can know everything. The lust for knowledge arises from the rationalistic assumption that if we know, then we can predict. And if we can predict, then we can control. This is the basis of the scientific commitment to take everything apart, to dissect in order to understand how a thing or a being ticks.

But here's the rub. In spite of the information revolution, we realize we can't know all that we need to know. So we outsource that work to others. We chafe at our child's poor academic performance, so we make an appointment with the school counselor. He sends us to a psychiatrist who can test for ADHD and prescribe medication. The psychiatrist is constrained by the demands of his profession to rely on the latest information from the drug company's sales rep. The drug representative selectively reports research findings that substantiate why his company's drug is the best option.

As long as we are attracted by the fantasy that knowledge delivers the power to control, we'll always be looking to the next study, expert, or groundbreaking finding to make life work. The problem is that there is no overarching authority to verify the truthfulness of any new piece of information. It's a jigsaw puzzle with an infinite-minus-one number of pieces and no unifying picture to guide us in putting the thing together. This sends many of us in one of two directions: either back to a simple, black-and-white dogmatism or to a hopeless agnosticism that says, "I don't know and I don't care!"

We know more about our children's developmental processes, psychological stresses, IQs, skill sets, temperaments, and emotional needs than any parents in history. Sadly, we know all about children, but we have lost sight of our child.

OMNIPOTENCE

The media offer the illusion of control through information, but our pursuit of this illusion leads only to exhaustion and confusion. If indeed we could be everywhere and know everything, then in theory we could also *do* anything.

The goal of presence and knowledge is to create, to make and shape life as we want it to be.

If one is omnipotent, then one doesn't suffer or do without; the omnipotent one is not hindered in any way. But if having access to information can't deliver this state, what can? In our culture, the means for achieving power is fame, or wealth, or both. The greater one's fame, the more power one possesses to name the terms of life and to rule over the chaos of uncertainty. The greater a person's wealth, the more she can insulate herself from uncertainty and numb the ache of life.

This connection between fame, wealth, and power helps explain our attraction to the media-created culture of celebrity. We watch the winner of a mega-lottery walk off with $90 million, or we see a man who can run faster, throw farther, and hit a ball better than anyone else sign a contract for tens of millions of dollars. It's not us, but it's someone. Figures from sports and entertainment and corporate America are our heroes. If their fame and wealth don't guarantee complete omnipotence, they sure tantalize us with the prospect that humans can enjoy nearly complete power and pleasure.

Our desire for omnipotence has us running in a circle: I wish I could be like the celebrities, exercising control over the chaos of life. But I can't, so I might as well enjoy as much pleasure as possible and try to avoid whatever makes me unhappy. Still, there is chaos. And the only control I can exercise is to try to gain more information about what's going on. So I switch on CNN, which means missing what my son or daughter is trying to tell me.

It's not simply that we have the television on too much. We do. And it's not that we listen to crass, godless music and watch repulsive movies. We do that, too. It's that we haven't faced our deep yearning for the media to be as wise and strong as God. When we seek power over our circumstances, we seek the omnipotence that only God possesses, and we lose the ability to hear his voice. And when we lose his voice, it's inevitable that we won't hear the voice of our children either.

I believe we will finally recognize the power of this idolatry when we see how friends, schools, and the church also deafen us to our children's voices.

Neighbors and Friends: Turning Down the Voice of Comparison

The stain of envy marks every neighborhood and all friendships. The writer of the book of Ecclesiastes tells us: "Then I observed that most people are motivated to success by their envy of their neighbors. But this, too, is meaningless, like chasing the wind."[1] We refer to this as "keeping up with the Joneses," but it runs a deeper and more insidious course than merely wanting to obtain whatever someone else buys.

The legacy of envy is the heavy burden of believing that our lot is lousy while everyone else's is sublime. The root of envy is the demand for heaven now, and the vehicle of envy is comparison. You have and I don't. I've felt that ache to possess when I hear friends describe the rest and intimacy they enjoyed during a fabulous trip. I feel it when I see a man in my neighborhood walking his kids to the bus stop and not rushing off to work because he is independently wealthy. I can even feel it when I hear a dear friend play the guitar and sing to the glory of God in a way that I can't. Envy is desire that aches with demand and is sodden with ingratitude.

Observe what happens when you see a commercial for a high-ticket item like a car. The people bounce to the beat of a classic rock song, and they have beatific grins on their faces. They are encased in a luxurious automotive haven that resists the storms and dangers of life because a personal genie waits at the touch of a button to tell them where they are and how much farther they can drive before having to stop for gas. I can't help but ask, "Why isn't *my* car like this?" I don't bop in ecstasy nor is there anyone to rescue me when I have a flat tire or get lost in a strange city.

Madison Avenue knows a car alone won't excite most people, so selling the product is actually selling an experience. We're buying the sizzle, not the steak. Marketing seeks to provoke need and then promise an easily achievable solution. We're familiar with this sales pitch, and we know it isn't true. So why do we keep falling for it?

The quick answer is that we can't help but fall for it. Advertisers are simply following the pattern of our stained hearts. We crave. We envy. And if we have those compulsions in the pursuit of time and money, then how much more so do we struggle with envy regarding our children?

ENVY AND OUR NEIGHBOR'S KID

A dear friend has a wonderfully talented daughter who excels in sports, academics, music, leadership, and spirituality. She is a state-ranked swimmer. She's an A+ student who loves math and science and who devours the classics. She sings beautifully and plays the violin. She is bright, beautiful, and most disconcerting of all, she is humble and winsomely unimpressed by her talent. I know that people like this exist; I just don't want to know them.

The parents are not arrogant when they extol their daughter's most recent accomplishments, but it's hard to respond with joy when she wins a state-wide science fair, and it took a life-and-death struggle to get my son to even acknowledge that he had a science project due on Monday. I love my children. I know God has equipped them specifically and perfectly for their calling. I know that envy is degrading and that it darkens gratitude and joy. I just don't like piano recitals, sports events, awards banquets, SAT scores, and all the assorted ways kids are compelled to compete against each other.

Some of the most blasphemous words out of my mouth toward my children have been, "Why can't you try harder like ———?" "How come Travis/Tiffany was invited to be on that team and you weren't?" and "Did you see how well dressed and polite Jennifer/Jeremy was at the wedding?" Comparing our child to another usually arises out of our dormant refusal to embrace who we are in God. And every comparison that is based on envy drowns out the voice of our child.

ENVYING OUR OWN CHILDREN

Envying other parents and children is often difficult to admit, but not hard to see. When we envy our own children, however, it is both difficult to admit and nearly impossible to see. How could I possibly envy my son or daughters? At times I merely envy their youth. At other times I compare myself as an eighth grader to my eighth-grade son and think, "I was such a dork, and he is so cool." He can play the trumpet, the didgeridoo, and the guitar, and I spent most of my time either eating Oreos or causing trouble in the neighborhood.

Envy, even in this case, seeps deeper into the soul. I've heard parents say, "I wish I'd had the benefits I've given my kid. It's just not fair." Usually that is said after a child has done something disappointing and made his parents' sacrifice seem foolish. Envy boils to the surface when we reject the sorrow that comes with parenting and instead resort to blame and regret.

A woman I worked with felt shame and envy when her daughter, who was born out of wedlock when the mother was only seventeen, became pregnant as a teenager. This mother had provided her daughter with plenty of love, a solid education, and a good church home. The daughter's pregnancy intensified not only the mother's anger and shame, but inflamed a brooding envy over the daughter's easy life compared to the mother's lonely and empty childhood.

We find ourselves envying our children's advantages, talent, beauty, strength, and poise. Knowing that the path of our life is largely set and their future is open, we can also envy their future. But envy of our children, on any level, can dull our senses to hearing their voice.

ENVYING THE EMPTY NESTER

We are apt to believe that our current stage of parenting is much more difficult than it will be in just a few years. I couldn't wait for the diaper days to wane so that the fun could begin. But then came the terrible twos and the thrilling threes—how would we survive? Just get us to kindergarten, and we'll have it made. Our habit of minimizing today while idolizing tomorrow is deeply ingrained.

One set of parents told me how excited they were that their last child was going off to college. They loved their kids, but they also looked forward to the quiet and to the rewards of more time together. They talked in rapt terms about projects they could finally finish, places they wanted to visit, and the rest they would enjoy after the wearying years of parenting.

I was lulled into counting how many years would pass before I could crow with such enthusiasm. The years extended past the fingers of one hand, and then I realized this empty-nest couple is my age. They were about to embark on the play days of life, and I still had to tell my son to turn his electric guitar down to 2.2 on the Richter scale. Balmy beaches and fruity drinks with paper parasols cavorted across my mind, and I had to snap the image off before I missed more of the conversation.

Moments after I returned from my little escape fantasy, the other couple mentioned their deep concerns about their oldest son who was struggling in his marriage. Their unmarried daughters were involved in less-than-ideal relationships with men the parents didn't respect. The son who was leaving for college was suffering anxiety attacks as he prepared to head off on his own. Then it dawned on me—once a parent, always a parent. The tie that binds will be broken only at death.

Envy in all forms dulls the heart and increases the noise that blocks our ability to listen to our children. The cure for envy is not to avoid the struggle of desire; far more, it is to recognize that envy is only a part of a bigger battle. The pressure that comes from our educational system intensifies the war.

Schools: Turning Down the Voice of Compulsion

Schools often are the beleaguered scapegoats of a culture that doesn't know what else to blame for society's woes. The ground-zero school that exposed our national vulnerability is Columbine. But the public education system at large has been under strain long before—and well after—the tragedy at Columbine.

CULTURE WARS GO TO SCHOOL

The educational milieu is saturated with conflicting values, ideologies, methodologies, and political machinations. No one questions whether it's important to teach reading, writing, science, and math. Nor would any ideology worth a moment's reflection argue that school is solely for learning basic skills. School has always been a socializing incubator that attempts to prepare children for good citizenship and economic productivity. The debate rages over the content and the process.

Somehow, the public education enterprise has bought into two core assumptions: the content must be value free, and the process must build self-esteem. If special value is assigned to a particular ideology, it affronts all other viewpoints. How can we teach Christian morality in a public school if we don't also make room for a Muslim, Buddhist, or even Wiccan perspective?

What has replaced any value or perspective is a neutered Golden Rule ethic—"Do unto others as you would have them do unto you."[2] The problem is that this biblical ethic for life has been redefined to position self-esteem as the bulwark against selfishness, greed, and cruelty. The foundation of education shifts from the conservative cry for content-driven curriculum and Judeo-Christian morality to the liberal accusation of authoritarianism and ideological imperialism. The liberal then argues for growth in critical thinking, tolerance, and self-esteem, to which the conservative decries the hypocrisy of supposed value-free humanism that infests children with a view of tolerance that makes it immoral to be opposed to homosexuality, premarital sex, or the self-esteem curriculum itself. Conservatives are branded as obstructionist, and liberals are labeled as hypocritically open to all ideologies and -isms except Christianity. Tolerance, it seems, has its limits.

Many parents don't care about these culture wars. But in our children's world, the din created by this debate is the creaking foundation underneath all the issues they face over homework, sex education, bullying, drinking, pre-marital sex, and the drug-based therapies being sold as the great panacea. Meanwhile, the bottom-line issue for most parents is whether their child is happy and getting good grades. Lost in the noise is the voice of our children telling us what their true needs are.

THE TENSION BETWEEN SECURITY AND RISK

No matter how hot the culture war becomes, the real demand from parents is that their children be happy and productive. Happiness means that the kids are not depressed or involved in harmful activities and that they feel good about themselves. Productivity is measured by grades good enough to get a student into the college of her choice so she can begin the long climb to financial independence. If a child stays out of trouble and develops decent learning skills, then parenting is little more than setting the aircraft on autopilot and occasionally checking the instruments.

But these parenting goals ignore the huge pressures the child is facing. Every teenager knows the pressure to conform to the rules and yet still stand out from everyone else. Kids also know too well the compulsion to succeed, but not be so smart that they lose connection with, and the respect of, their peers. The pressure for parents is to push the child to succeed without dis-couraging him or diminishing his self-esteem. We can't have an unhappy child, but neither can we abide a slacker. Either way, the child is under pressure.

The problem for parents, kids, and school systems alike is the tension between safety and danger, between security and risk. The greater the de-mand for success, the less safety there can be. The more we measure grades and performance in a competitive environment, the higher the potential for some children to suffer from poor self-esteem. A good example is the grade-school reading group. Do you mix high-level and low-level readers? If so, then the entire group will be slowed to the pace of the weakest link. If, how-ever, the group is divided according to ability, then those assigned to the low-level group will be esteem-challenged. It is a simple principle of life: One must choose either more safety or greater risk. As in financial investments, if you seek a higher rate of return, the risk level goes up.

The fatal flaw of the self-esteem movement is that we can't have the optimum of both worlds simultaneously. We must favor either risk or safety, or settle for the boring average—achieving neither great performance nor exceptional stability. This muddy middle ground is what the school systems have achieved. The result is an average, not highly distinctive product, and the pressure remains on kids to find a way to rise above the homogenized masses.

Never before has there been an age where *being average* is so hated and striven against. Never have more extracurricular activities been part of the menu. My wife and I spend untold hours driving our children to soccer, music lessons, youth group, tennis tournaments. We are being crushed under the pressure to help our children succeed. It is hard for parents to hear the voice of their children when we've been yelling at them to finish their homework so that we can rush them to the *n*th event of the week. And then, to top it off, church looms on Sunday.

Church: Turning Down the Voice of Conformity

It might surprise you that the church often keeps us from listening to our children. It should be enough that the media, our neighbors and friends, and the schools create more than enough noise to drown out our children's voices. The church should be a place not only of quiet, but also of freedom to admit and wrestle with our deepest struggles—unless, of course, the church is seen as the cultural mediator of morality rather than as the safe refuge for sinners. For many, a safer refuge is a bar, the hair salon, or the health club. In those places everyone knows your dreams and feels compelled to put up with your idiosyncrasies, providing at least a faux-structure of acceptance. In the church, however, we often encounter gossip and judgment. Certainly these offenses are suffered as well in other venues, but when they occur in the church, they violently contradict the heart of redemption.

A COMMUNITY OF STANDARDS

The Bible is chock-full of standards and commands. A believer is not to produce the fruits of the flesh. We are not to be drunk nor compromise our sexual purity. We are not to be under the control of any object, person, or idea other than our love of God. But we are.

No human, past or present, other than Jesus, has the passion and purity to obey the Father completely. We all fall short. Falling short means that every single moment of our life, we need grace. Without God's forgiveness we can't stand against his judgment.

In fact the church is both the celebrator of grace and the poet of holiness. It is not an error for Christians to live righteous lives or to strive to live out the fruit of the Holy Spirit in their private lives as well as in the broader culture. But we fail when certain standards of behavior, rather than grace and forgiveness, are assumed to be the core of Christianity. The heart of our faith is not a set of rules, but the Cross. The result of a standards-oriented religion is the rise, if not the dominance, of a self-righteousness for those who appear to be doing what is expected. For those who aren't as adept at deceiving others, the outcome of a standards-driven Christianity will be shame.

A COMMUNITY OF SHAME

Shame is the experience of being exposed and judged. I may feel awkward disrobing in front of a physician, but if he says, "Wow, you're really fat!" my awkwardness will turn to shame and fury. A community of shame can be as brusque as outright shunning, but most congregations resort to a more insidious form—gossip. If it weren't for "Christian concern" communicated in the form of gossip, we'd all be free to stand during a prayer service and ask for help regarding the struggles we're experiencing with a willful teenager.

There are three reasons that we don't ask for help when the tension is still live and threatening to undo us. First, if we did, we'd be one of a very few who has *ever* publicly shared something that is personal and unresolved. Second, we'd find people avoiding us. And the few who speak would either offer sweet but ineffective concern or recommend a book, a prayer, or even a rebuke. For a person who is struggling, asking openly for help is like hanging a bull's-eye on their back and then handing out ammunition. Third, our struggle would become the fodder for conversation. One might as well take out a public notice in the local newspaper: "Edward 'Smitty' Smith announces that he and his son, Eddie Jr., have endured multiple outbursts of anger and heightened tension. Edward further acknowledges that he handled his fury by turning self-righteous, inflaming his son with groundless accusations. Then Edward withdrew into a holier-than-thou silent treatment, which really annoyed fifteen-year-old Eddie. Edward admits his error and requests prayer from the entire community."

The church was established as the place of grace, the one sanctuary where we should be free to honestly admit our weakness and failure. But in practice it's the place where we are most likely to hide our flaws from others. Sadly, we replace a quest for grace with a charade of conformity.

THE COMMUNITY OF CONFORMITY

The goal of many who attend church is to get something from God without being found out by people. Of course there are people who attend church to make business contacts in the same way they would as a member of a social club. But the vast majority of people attend hoping to gain spiritual meaning or a moment of connection to God.

Equally represented are those seeking safety and stability, those who want an endorsement of how they are living rather than encouragement to embrace the bold risk of the life of faith. These people are similar to those who hit the ski slopes not to enjoy the exhilaration of barreling downhill atop two thin blades of fiberglass, but in hopes of reaching the bottom of the slope without falling on their backsides. It's not hard to pick out the safe skiers. Their stance is stiff and their movement slow and plodding. Their turns lack openness and elegance. In the same way, some go to church to better get through the week, but they are not there to aim the pointy ends downhill and to engage the agony and ecstasy of pursuing God.

Likewise, parents fall into the trap of working hard not to fail rather than passionately pursuing God's leading in the lives of their children. The parent who is governed by a regimen of rules and responsibility is the parent whose primary hope is to raise morally upright children. Period. *If school is to make my son smart and competent,* this parent thinks, *then church is responsible for helping my child become good and responsible.*

Many will protest: "Of course I want my child to be good, but far more I want my son or daughter to know Jesus as Lord and Savior and to live for his purposes." Fair enough. But what if your child loves the Lord and also wants to have her nose pierced? What if she wants to live in the inner city and give her life to walking alongside spiritually impoverished prostitutes and drug addicts? What if your son is led by his faith to view the conservative political enterprise as bereft of courage and mercy and thus aligns himself with a faith-based social action agency?

Helping our children come to know Jesus is only the first step. The bigger pursuit is that we want them to follow God without compromise. We want them to catch the passion of living boldly and taking big risks as in following God. Try to find a key figure in the Bible, other than Jesus, who followed God without compromise and who was also anything other than a wreck. God's most ardent disciples, in both the Old and New Testament, are not those whose lives unfold neatly and progress in a straight line. His boldest followers are burdened people, the targets of public opposition, often conflicted within themselves, and seldom the pride of their village or even their faith community. Are we really willing to let our children take big risks and fail at profound and ghastly levels if God uses such failure to draw their hearts to him?

I ask myself that question fairly regularly, and I confess that in the heat of the parenting battle, I usually just want my kids to behave. They know the rules; I just want them to comply. But they will not do as I wish, let alone as I demand. Their choices often conflict with my desires, which evokes the noise of fear, shame, anger, hurt, and confusion as I merely think about my children, let alone actually talk and listen to them.

Our task is not to find a way to be freed once and for all from this godless noise—the voices of the media, friends, school, and even the church. God merely invites us to confess that we are deaf and that our ears and eyes must be opened so we can engage our children. Only by learning to silence the competing voices will we ever gain the wisdom that comes from listening to our children.

CHAPTER 6

Hearing the Voice of Your Marriage

The Music of a Godly Union

T here is one central point so far: Too many other voices are drowning out the voices of our children. One of the saddest sounds that distorts our capacity to listen to the true questions, accusations, and desires of our children is the noise coming from our marriage. Often it is the noise of unresolved tensions. It also can be the noise of silence when two partners separate and divorce.

No sound is meant to produce music that soothes and shapes the life of a child more than the voice of his or her parents' marriage. Conversely, no sounds can more horribly silence a child than the noise of a troubled and unrepentant marriage. So far we've tried to hear and silence the voices of our parents, friends, the media, school, and church to keep them from dulling our hearing. Now we plunge into the most important task of all: to face how the words of our marriages either drown out or invigorate the voices of our children.

The Model Marriage

God intends marriage to be the one relationship that most deeply reveals his character, heart, passion, and purpose. A marriage is the face of God to a world that can't see him unless he is portrayed in human flesh. Marriage embodies God's Trinitarian nature through the interaction and union of distinct and complementary persons. Marriage can and should mirror God's strength and mercy. Marriage, in all honesty, is also a mess.

The model marriage reveals God's character, and it also exposes our profound need for forgiveness. Just as marriage is meant to reveal something of God's *hesed,* or covenantal love, it is also the deepest proof of our need for God's loyal love because of the tide of sin and sorrow that rises in every marriage. The most intense, profound, and eternal issues of life surface in the context of two human beings committing their futures together and telling every destructive force and influence that nothing but death will ever divide them. If it seems that this is a brash invitation for problems to grow, that's exactly what it is.

Marriage is the moist soil that grows both the weeds of sin and the roses of redemption. No other relationship requires more, gives so little and so much, and exposes both the best and the worst of our souls. Every weakness in one's character—a lack of patience, a fear of intimacy, an unnatural clinging to grudges—will be magnified. Wonderfully, the most hidden and unformed depths of sacrifice and perseverance also rise at the most unexpected moments in a good marriage.

It is crucial to state the next point with brazen clarity: Children need to see the best and the worst of a marriage in order to understand not only the depth of sin, but also the luminescent glory of conviction, repentance, grace, reconciliation, and celebration. Otherwise relational darkness will be known but not named. And it will poison the hope of healing.

During the poverty of our graduate school days, my wife and I used to go out to eat once a week after church. We were too poor to both order a meal, and so each week we would alternate who got to order. Then we'd split the meal. One week we both argued that it was our turn. Our voices were rising and taking on the intensity of both conviction and hunger. It was not a harsh interaction, but in the midst of our debate we heard our two-year old Annie say, "Money, money, money. All you ever fight about is money."

I thought we were going to choke with laughter until the weight of her insight hit us. Children often intuit what we refuse to see. What if we actually listened to their voices? How might our marriages change, and in turn how different might we be as parents?

What a paradoxical stance. A parent must reveal God and his grace not only by modeling what is true, but also what is false. Thankfully, none of us will need to fail on purpose; it will be both natural and frequent. But when sin arises it must not be swept aside as a parental prerogative or a mere aberration. Marriage is the training ground for the truest and most risky pursuit of maturity, so it must be conducted in full view of our children.

The Mockery of Marriage

There are three great violations of marriage—divorce, indifference, and abuse. In all three cases marriage is mocked, and dark laughter from the bowels of hell dulls and distorts the hearts of the children who are wounded by the fallout.

DIVORCE AND THE HATRED OF HOPE

Divorce is a living death. When a parent dies, the relationship continues only in memory and dream. There is no present to add to the storehouse of relationship. Death creates a static, unresolved-yet-resolved ending that eventually evokes both gratitude for what was given and an ache for what was missed. Hope regarding the parent who has died becomes a fluid part of the greater hope of the Day of the Lord, when justice will reign and reconciliation will be not only personal but also cosmic. These same things are *not* true, however, for the child who wrestles with a hatred of hope in the midst of a divorce.

Every child of divorced parents dreams of the day when Mom and Dad will come back together. They just might come to their senses and reunite. The child is living the torture of a double bind. If he stops hoping, then something in his heart must die. If he continues to hope, he is prey to the vicissitudes of desire. In either case, it is a double death—either one that is climactic, final, and harsh, or the other that is a death by degrees, slowly spaced apart so that each feels like a new, cruel torture.

The roller-coaster ride of hope aroused and then deferred leaves the heart of the child sick.[1] It's much easier to kill the hope than to bear its periodic arousal followed always by decline. Divorce is not merely a disaster in the present; it is arson of the past and the assassination of the future. The good times remembered are now impossible to recall without a sense of intense loss. The burned past blows away in dark ash, and the future is killed to avoid the temptation of renewed hope.

Divorce leaves children with contempt toward intimacy and loyalty. Intimacy is viewed as the seductress that lures one into love. But those children now know that nothing good can last, so intimacy is the lure of a lie—better to leave before the end descends. Divorce brings cynicism, and the children form relationships that refuse to surrender to the other's good, while at the same time exploiting intimacy through sexuality and casual pseudocommitment.

No one thinks divorce is a great societal good. Many would say it is, at best, a sad and inevitable necessity. The bottom line is that divorce presents an enormous challenge to a parent who is already reeling from the loss, faced now with the financial and personal demands of single parenting and in need of healing while also providing for the emotional well-being of the children. Divorce requires the highest demand at the worst possible moment—and it can be done, but not to anyone's satisfaction.

To quiet the noise of divorce, a parent needs the allies of time, heroic patience, and a disquieting openness to how a child will sabotage hope. Sadly, many divorced parents destabilize the child's intimacy with the other parent and pretend life is normal—or at least better than it was. The child ends up being a pawn of angry parental politics and learns the skills of disinterested manipulation.

When a divorce is amicable, the tensions are less severe, but the noise of confusion and the hatred of hope will be just as high. On one hand the child says, "If someone as smart as Mom can make such a bad mistake, then how can I avoid the same fate?" The result will be a deep-seated doubt that any relationship can last, let alone be good and true. On the other hand, if the child says, "Mom married a loser because she's a loser, and I won't make the same stupid mistake," the child will grow to be presumptuous and arrogant.

Going through a divorce and still choosing to hear the heart of one's child requires immense courage and conviction. It requires a willingness to step even deeper into the child's ambivalence, blame, and fear—and to do so with the conviction that, as the process humbles us, we will grow, and in turn, our hurting child will grow.

INDIFFERENCE AND THE FEAR OF BOREDOM

There is a strong, almost shrill demand among many that, no matter what, troubled couples need to stay together—for the good of the children. The marriage may be awful, and one or both partners may be miserable, but even a bad marriage is better for the kids than divorce. This remains to be seen. And being asked to decide is like being asked if you'd like to commit suicide by drowning or an overdose. Which of these is the more humane way to do harm? A choice such as this is not a true choice.

Instead the real choice is between risking a higher degree of tension—and possibly even divorce—by *refusing* to remain indifferent. Such a refusal means taking the risk to turn indifference into intimacy, or possibly estrangement. It is a sad fact that some intact marriages might end if one partner chose to pursue the other in kindness, honesty, and passion. A number of marriages are sustained merely by convenience or conformity or by the comfort born of sustained, mutual distaste. When challenged to grow, many of these misshapen unions collapse with that slightest additional weight. The relationship is like a woven lawn chair that has been left out in the weather too long and becomes brittle. It is intact, but at the first added weight it sags and eventually snaps. The fallout for children who grow up amid the noise of such an indifferent marriage is a sense that marriage holds no hope for intimacy, joy, and pleasure. Marriage is seen as a boring, monotone relationship that is no match for drugs, sex, and rock'n'roll.

Indifference is a form of passive-aggressive hatred. There are many who know the cry, "Love me or hate me! Just don't ignore me!" I've spoken with many African-Americans who would rather face the clear contempt of a bigot than the eyes of a person who looks through them without even seeing their face. Indifference implies you are not worth my anger or hurt, let alone my deeper desire. It says, "You don't even exist, let alone matter."

Marital indifference comes in many forms. There are couples who live such distant lives that physical or verbal touch is unheard of. As long as the family duties are well structured, this home can run smoothly with little overt unhappiness. Children in these families grow up in something of an antiseptic lab that prizes Prussian efficiency and order rather than intimate connection. The result in their lives will be a craving for intimacy and a flight from mechanical indifference.

Another form of indifference is role compartmentalization. Men watch football; women cook meals. Men talk politics; women talk recipes, fashion, and babies. Men are tough; women are tender. Period. There are many homes where role differentiation is sufficiently severe that the husband and wife exist on the border of the other with very little overlap. Often a low level of contempt toward the opposing sex magnifies the distance. The result in the lives of children will be a fear of crossing boundaries and a hatred of being locked into only one mode of being.

Perhaps the most common form of indifference is seen in the couple that settles for getting along and establishing a positive disposition in the family. I call this the Disneyland marriage. There is no trash on the streets and no disorder to be seen. Everyone is expected to be happy and have fun. And because the price for not being happy is too great, the normal struggles of growing up and coming to terms with life are kept safely out of sight.

This couple can be merry and fun. Very often a relaxed, companionable feeling permeates the home. If this picture is starting to look pretty good to you, consider that the indifference in this marriage is evident in the avoidance of depth. There is a refusal to allow the unhappiness of life to compel anyone to ask, seek, or knock. The provisions of life are readily available, so why ask tough questions, engage in meaningful dialogue, or live with the tension of uncertainty and doubt? This family knows black from white and eschews the gray. The indifference to tension, confusion, and sorrow makes it necessary to glide on the surface. Any movement toward depth in a conversation would require both parties to face the reality of darkness and unhappiness, and they're just not willing to go there.

The result is a family in which no one really listens or bothers to ask. There is no reason to raise issues of deep concern because anything other than happy chatter is akin to passing gas—an impolite and inappropriate expression. The consequence in the lives of the children is either an unhealthy avoidance of disrupting the status quo or a terrible, dark desire to flout social conventions.

All three forms of marital indifference leave the heart of a child craving action, depth, and meaning. A child needs to witness the truth of intimacy and relationship. Godly parents are called to end the false truce of indifference and open the door to potential conflict, contempt, and carnage. It is not righteous to endure an indifferent marriage and spawn in your children a contempt toward intimacy and a fear of boredom. Parents must not deprive their children of the fruits of suffering and risk. The price of shunning risk is growing deaf to your children's cry for real life.

ABUSE AND THE SEEDS OF VIOLENCE

The expression "abusive marriage" is not a mere oxymoron. It is a fiendish violation of God's kind intention in bringing two humans into union. Abuse is the murder of personhood. It is abhorrent to God, the marital equivalent of the damage wrought by false teachers described in the Bible as savage wolves who arise and devour the flock.[2] When a husband who is called to be the head of a family instead devours his wife and children in rage and emotional assaults, if he physically humiliates them, or if he stains their innocence through sexual abuse, there is an element of rage in God's righteous anger. Such a husband and father is violating not only a child's body but also that child's trust in God, which typically leads to rage, self-destructive habits, and violence later in life.[3]

Abuse in its most raw and overtly violent forms—rape and other types of physical harm—is condemned in our society. Lesser forms of abuse, such as touching another person's genitals and physical abuse that extends only to bruises or welts, is still condemned, but legal prosecution is rare. Likewise, neglect and intermittent physical harm are viewed as aberrant but not worthy of intervention or legal consequences. So those who commit much of the abuse against children are never brought to justice. Instead the most common forms of abuse are hidden under a cover of shame, and the children suffer serious, ongoing harm without recourse.

A woman I worked with was married to a demeaning and violent man. He required his wife to take a job outside the home to provide financial support. He also demanded that she do all the housework. He spent his time on investment research that theoretically would enhance the family's income, but in fact he only lost the money that his wife earned. When she asked him to get a full-time job, he balked and accused her of being cold and unsubmissive. She cowed to his abuse and indeed grew in shame, resentment, and hurt.

This continued for years until she came to her senses and refused to continue working. Her husband began to verbally pound on her to return to work, and the abuse was extended to some of the children. The children who aligned with their mother were harmed physically and emotionally by the father. The children who sided with their father were rewarded and given the freedom to do as they wished.

The woman eventually went to her pastor and asked for prayer and intervention. The pastor refused to step into the mess because the man was known for being fractious and divisive. Later the pastor, in a fit of conscience, admitted that he was afraid the man might sue him or the church if he initiated an accountability process or any church discipline. Purely on a cost-benefit basis, the pastor and church leadership didn't believe they had the resources, nor the congregational support, to expose, discipline, and disciple a misogynist. Instead it was easier to confront the one who was most open to God, the abusive man's wife, and enjoin her to trust that God would change her husband's heart if she would just do what he wanted.

God hates divorce, and he opposes those in power who devour the sheep and refuse to stop the carnage that comes with the abuse of power in a relationship.[4] These sheep endure brutal men and women who wreak untold harm. And then we allow these brutal people to avoid our scrutiny and to escape consequences because doing something doesn't seem worth the enormous effort of assessment, evaluation, and intervention.

But thankfully, this scenario is not always the case. There are faith communities that, with grace and strength, come alongside an angry man. In one church I know, an abusive man was required to be part of an anger-management group. He was invited to see a good therapist, and his wife was given avenues of escape if his rage became debilitating to the family. In a brilliant and kind fashion, the church stepped in to say, "Yes, you are loved. And no, you can't get your own way."

Sadly, it's easier to fix the spotlight on sexual immorality and rage against it than to expose emotional, physical, and sexual abuse that is finally reported by a victimized wife. We have no problem telling teenagers to say no to premarital sex, but we're too eager to say maybe to an abusive husband.

There is no gray area here. Abuse is any situation that does severe harm on an emotional, physical, or sexual level. That is unequivocally true. On the other hand, I've had the privilege of working with wickedly dysfunctional families that have been open to profound and significant exposure and change. The number is small, but it's wrong to assume that all violent homes and people are beyond the capacity to change. The church must call men and occasionally women to responsibility for creating a dark world of violence and then help them name and accept the privilege of creating a tender and strong home. The fact that some change must compel us to invite *all* who are abusive to change.

After all, what does an abusive family do to the heart of a child? The simplest answer is that abuse sows the seeds of violence for the next genera-tion. Violence creates a perpetrator-victim relationship that will *always* be supplanted by the victim becoming the perpetrator (in some fashion) and recreating the dynamic for more children in the future. Love is the only anti-dote to a cycle that has evolved since the mayhem of Cain and Abel.

Having examined the homes that shout down the voices of children, let's now move to the kind of home that hears children and invites them into the arms of God.

The Music of a Godly Marriage

Wherever parents fail to grow as human beings, we also refuse that growth opportunity for our children. We can't take our children any farther in life, relationship, and love than the point we have chosen to progress on our own and in our marriages. But if marriage is to bear the marks of holiness that will invite children to become what they are meant to be, it must suffer three core issues. These issues involve the complexity of sin and redemption, freedom and responsibility, and intimacy and independence. These irresolvable conun-drums do not bow to a linear, black-and-white, easy-answer mentality. They demand the willingness to live in the midst of tension. They require that we struggle well and that we deeply surrender to a Person, not to some quick-fix formula.

SIN AND REDEMPTION

The tension between sin and redemption is to name both the ongoing, staggering blight of darkness in my soul even as I am surrounded and penetrated by the glory of the light of Christ. It is not an either/or but a both/and stance. I am both light and dark; alive and dead; sinful and redeemed. This stance allows me to face more deeply all that is left to be redeemed in my being, while not denying the glory of what has been revealed to me and done within me.

A godly marriage acknowledges that no one is more loved, or more hated, than one's spouse. The hatred does not eviscerate love, nor does my spouse's love entirely eradicate my need for even more complete and life-changing redemption. A godly marriage becomes the central proving ground that God is at work. If the marriage merely survives or if it spirals into emotional estrangement or aggravated violence, then there is no good soil in which to grow the fruit of redemption in one's children.

Parents must have the ability to confess to their children what every child knows intuitively—there is a failure of love in the family. It is idiotic to think that our children don't see what we work so hard to hide. It didn't take too many encounters with my kids for them to know and name that I am prone to foolish anger.

At age six my middle child, Amanda, said to me as we stood in line at an amusement park, "Daddy, I know we're having to wait longer than you like. Will you promise me you won't yell at someone, especially me?" I felt weak before her utterly sweet, innocent, and sharp-witted awareness. Her words—and many since then—have haunted me and invited me to more quickly (still not as often or as fast as I desire) face my failure.

If we parents can't first confess our failures of love to our spouse, there is small likelihood that we will name them in the larger family matrix. In fact, how we confess to our most intimate partner will set the standard for how we name sin with everyone else. We must also have the ability to confess to our children that there is real hope for love in brokenness. It's one thing to admit failure. (Some do so with such frequency and pathetic demand, it's almost worse than not admitting failure at all.) But to confess failure, truly, is to hunger for redemption.

And redemption is not merely change, nor is it knowing that one is forgiven. There are some who change only to become proud and demanding of others to do the same. Others know they are forgiven and use that as an excuse to perpetrate the same harm again and again, expecting no personal consequences. True redemption involves being struck dumb by the enormity of our failure and then struck even dumber by the enormity of the heart of God that cancels our debt. Redemption brings a level of gratitude that frees the heart to desire the sweet balm of forgiveness for oneself and others. It frees the heart to extend to others what has been so freely given to us.

Redemption is the soil that enables our children to see our failures and therefore face their own. Redemption also moves an entire family to a level of kindness and honesty where they are unafraid to wrestle with the core issues of our souls.

FREEDOM AND RESPONSIBILITY

Life is fraught with constant conundrums of choice. We have, for instance, the freedom to choose virtually anything, but we can't escape the responsibility that comes with choice, namely that every choice we make brings with it a sure consequence.

In marriage there is a choice about who mows the lawn and who cooks the meals. Most of the time that choice is tied to our assumptions about gender roles. The majority of homes put grass cutting into the hands of the man and serving dinner into the care of the woman. For many families, this arrangement is a good fit with the primary interests of the husband and wife, but it's not a matter of necessity or a requirement of gender-determined aptitude.

Who does what is a choice, and it is shortsighted to assume that there are no consequences related to this choice. If the division of labor is attributed to predetermined gender roles, then children are left to assume that all men cut lawns and all women prefer to cook. And though this issue is relatively minor, it sets in place a larger structure of assumptions that has little to do with what God wants to reveal through the radical differences that he wove into gender.

How a husband and wife define and negotiate choice—from who does what around the house to where the family will vacation and how limited supplies of money and time will be allocated—are the raw fodder that allows children to grapple with the glory and horror of choice. If children don't see their parents in this tension, they won't be prepared for choice, and they will come to despise the weight of freedom as they grow older.

Too many of us blindly adopt cultural norms without reflection or intention. Whether the culture is a local church or the larger media culture, we frequently define what is good and right according to what is most acceptable to others. When our children oppose such conformity, they are challenging norms that have little to do with the heart issues of the Bible. If we confuse culturally defined roles with biblical requirements, for instance, then our children's choices that differ from the norm will be considered rebellious. We'll wrongly try to steer them toward fitting into the culture rather than toward adherence to biblical requirements. We actually sow seeds of divisiveness in our children's future relationships when we buy into the culture's demands rather than seeking God's standards for marriage.

The realities of sin and salvation force us to face what is true about both our internal world and the world beyond what we can see. Freedom and responsibility compel us to grapple with the nearly infinite array of choices and the inevitability of the consequences that follow the choices we make. Meanwhile, intimacy and independence call attention to the way we bridge the internal world of desire and the external world of relationships and achievement.

INTIMACY AND INDEPENDENCE

We can't escape the tension that arises between intimacy and independence. Intimacy is the delight one finds in connection with another. In intimacy we find rest and stability. But we are made for more than being at rest while enjoying closeness to another. We also are made to experiment, risk, and explore the unknown. We're as much made to be independent as we are made to be intimate. Independence calls us to live out the call on our life both in spite of and in light of our commitment to others. It's the tension that is often felt in this choice: "Shall I do what *I* want to do, or shall I do what will make *you* happy?" When it's taken to a higher level, the question is asked in these terms: "Shall I do what I feel called and what I long to do, or shall I do what promises to bring me the greatest amount of approval from those I love?"

Every choice for intimacy sacrifices some independence, and every choice to be independent costs us a portion of intimacy. If I remain at home today to finish writing this chapter, I lose the opportunity to go on a hike with my family. If I go with my family and enjoy the conviviality and surprises of a day in the mountains, then I'll fall behind on a writing task that depends entirely on my operating as an individual. (I went hiking.)

The tension between intimacy and individuality requires each of us to honestly name and then choose how much intimacy and independence we desire at any one moment. This discussion can't occur with regard to children unless parents address it. Are we free to differ with each other on significant matters without losing the joy of connection? Are we free to fail one another without fearing the loss of relationship? Can we *both* be right (or wrong) in a conversation without demanding that one viewpoint overshadow the other? If not, then independence will always exact the high cost of loss of relationship.

For example, what if I can't bear to allow my wife to pursue the dreams that line up with the passions of her life? What if she senses that God is calling her to be more involved in caring for the elderly, and that would mean committing much more of her time to this pursuit? Meanwhile, I want her to pursue a more flexible schedule so we can take more vacations to relieve the stress of my work. Her passion competes with my desire. Whose desire will take preeminence? How will that decision be made? Can one spouse grow in the calling to be oneself (independence) in a way that is compatible with being in relationship (intimacy)?

The answers to these questions depend to a large degree on how we live out the issues of sin and redemption. What if it's assumed that neither my spouse nor I really sin or truly need redemption? Perhaps we acknowledge sin as failure with a casual nod, and we regard redemption only as a one-time, accomplished fact. From now on, as long as we're pretty good about doing the right things, there's not really much to talk about.

If that's the perspective, the issues of sin and redemption aren't dealt with in a practical and consistent form. Neither do we get to the core of what's going on in the life of each family member. No wonder child rearing in homes such as this is far less concerned about the child's heart and far more concerned about rules and conformity. More accurately said, parenting with this mind-set is really the exertion put forth to keep a child doing well in school, the neighborhood, church, and sports, rather than going all out in pursuit of God and his purposes.

Such a family simply falls into roles prescribed by religious and cultural authorities. And if choice and responsibility are largely turned over to what others tell us, then it is unlikely there will be an openness to listen to our children if what they claim to feel differs from what we assume they "ought" to feel. Parents' ability to listen to their child is dependent on what they are willing to hear. If I am deaf to the complex issues of intimacy and independence because the "authorities" have said parenting is merely a matter of following certain rules, then I will not hear my child's cry to engage in the mess that is within them.

To help, let me offer an illustration. When my daughter Amanda was in the fourth grade, she was told by a friend that she couldn't come over to play because the girl was going to another friend's birthday party. This child knew that Amanda hadn't been invited. My daughter was overwhelmed with sadness. My wife was solicitous and comforting. After a time I felt like her sorrow flowed into a demand for a relief that was impossible to supply.

I'm more inclined to the stance of tough-it-out. It's my sinful proclivity to flee from tears and demand action. I know it's not right to ignore my daughter's tears simply on the basis of my own bias. On the other hand life is unfair, and we are free to choose what we do with loss. We can weep in sorrow, or we can do something about life's unfairness.

Amanda wanted comfort, but her tears hid a deep strain of vengeance. I needed to hear her and then respond to her deepest questions, accusations, and desires. But I didn't want to expend the time. I was sorely tempted to offer a few patronizing words of comfort while ignoring her pain and unnamed anger. Why was I backing off—laziness, fear of her response, uncertainty about what to do, a demand that life be easier than it is? The answer was enough of each that if I wanted to love my daughter, I had to do more.

In that flashing moment, I was making a decision about intimacy and independence. If I engaged Amanda, it would take away from my plans and set me into the possible debacle of alienating my wife and/or daughter. I had a choice: pursue my previous plans for the hour or respond freely to my daughter's need of the moment. I chose to succumb to intimacy and the loss of independence.

I sat next to Amanda and said in a voice louder than her tears, "I am so angry at Sarah that I'm going to go to her party and knock over her cake." Amanda turned her eyes toward me, but her arms and body were still tied to her mother. I said, "No, I'm not. I'm going to go over there and take her cake and all her presents." At this point Amanda laughed. It was all I needed to know that we were onto something. I asked her, "Do you want to go with me? We can put on masks so they won't know who we are. We'll break into the party, knock over the drinks, and steal the cake and presents. That'll teach her not to mess with Amanda Allender!"

Amanda looked at me with 20 percent seriousness and said, "Really?" I laughed and asked if she really wanted me to do it. She said, "Not really, but sort of." Now the conversation was moving. She was no longer crying, nor was she laughing. She was curious. What I told her was brief and simple: "Amanda, when I'm hurt, I often want someone to pay. But not only does making someone pay add to their pain, but it always comes back to make me even more miserable. I'm glad you can admit you are hurt and angry, and I'm even more glad you're willing to see that revenge is not what you really want. So stop crying, kid, and help me clean up the garage."

I have no idea what that conversation did for her. I don't know if she even remembers it. I do know that my wife was tickled, Amanda was happier, we got some work done that afternoon, and the sorrow of life neither silenced us nor defeated us.

Every marriage is the proving ground for wrestling with the deepest matters of the heart. If one spouse refuses to hear the matters of eternity in the marriage relationship, it's unlikely that he or she will be able to do so as a parent. The level of our grappling, and the depth of our honesty in confronting life as it is in our marriages, will determine our ability to guide our children into an honest pursuit of God and his purposes. That's the music and the power of a godly marriage.

CHAPTER 7

Living in the Heart
of Mystery

How We Give Our Children a Taste of God's Character

G iven the noise that surrounds us, it's a wonder that we're able to hear our children at all. But they are always speaking to us, and we can always do a better job hearing them. It's not enough to say that there's too much other noise or to simply name the different sources of the cacophony. The noise of the world is endless, and although it conspires against our success as parents, the task is far from hopeless.

Early in my years of parenting, I had the opportunity to interact with a great theologian, William Hendrickson. Dr. Hendrickson was in his eighties when I met him over lunch with a number of other young pastors. He was a devout man who had written nine New Testament commentaries. In a passing moment, between sipping iced tea and eating a tuna sandwich, he astounded all of us. "I think I am just beginning to get a grasp of the gospel," he acknowledged.

How could he have written all those commentaries and now say he was just beginning to grasp the gospel? I'd been in the ministry for only a year, and I certainly had more than a beginning handle on the good news of God. Either Dr. Hendrickson was losing it, or I was presumptuous and arrogant. But his remark—and one he made later—struck something deeper in me than my arrogance.

The young pastors around the table began talking about the huge demands we felt as fathers. Dr. Hendrickson smiled and said, "Remember, parenting is not difficult; it is impossible." His laugh conveyed both agony and hope. He answered a few more questions, then before our time with him ended, he returned to the subject of parenting. He looked at us young men and said, "Nothing you do will be more important than being fathers, and in nothing will you fail more miserably. Parenting is impossible, so you will need God more than [you will need to be] a good parent."

I couldn't predict at that moment how deeply those words would take root inside me. I can't comprehend all that I fail to grasp about the gospel, let alone the vast stores of God's truth about life. But I'm beginning to fathom the truth of Dr. Hendrickson's second statement: I'm not as good a father as I desire to be, and I know parenting is not something someone fully masters. It is life's most exacting, ambiguous, life-consuming calling. And it is utterly and completely impossible. It is impossible in part because we finite, fallible creatures are called to reveal to our children the infinite, pure character of God. We can't fathom all that God has given to us, so how can we hope to offer the same to our children? And yet that is what we've been called to do. In fact, our task is nothing less than to give our children a taste of God's character.

The Gift of God's Character

Parenting is more than burping a child or providing for the high costs of college. It is more than soccer parenting or suffering the interminable humiliations of a piano recital. A parent may do all the above or none of the above and either be a great or an awful parent. The true goal of parenting is to introduce a child to God—and I don't mean simply steering the child toward praying the sinner's prayer. A parent's calling is to daily reflect God's character into the life of the child. The dilemma, of course, is that God is difficult to find even for those of us who have known him for decades.

The apostle Paul provided the answer we need. Our invisible God chooses to make himself visible in his creation, through such things as stars, slugs, songs, and parents.[1] God is eager to use all created things and beings, no matter how lowly, to reveal his character. However, he uniquely reveals himself as a person. And as a person, he bears two unique and apparently contradictory qualities: He is tender and merciful, and he is strong and full of wrath. Adding to the impossibility of the task of parenting is that we are called to reveal God in equal measure both in mercy and in strength.

The psalmist offered one of the shortest theologies in the Bible when he wrote, "You, O God, are strong, and…you, O Lord, are loving."[2] God holds us accountable for our wrongdoing (strength), yet he also provides the full amount necessary to cover the debt of our disobedience (love and mercy). He demands that we obey his law (strength) and then sends his perfect sacrifice, the unblemished lamb of God, his Son, to pay the penalty for our rebellion (mercy). God's strength provides the order and organization of life—setting the boundary between water and land, night and day—whereas his mercy invites us to play and create in his creation. In strength and tenderness God leads us into deeper union with him, just as the first couple knew, walking safely and freely in the cool of the day. The trouble is that we live nowhere near the Garden of Eden.

Outside the garden, God's strength and mercy seem to be in conflict. His righteous, holy strength will not come into the presence of impurity; and yet his tender heart can't resist running to the impure sinner. God is in conflict with his creation and in his own urges of strength and mercy.

God says,

Is not Ephraim my dear son, the child in whom I delight? Though I often speak against him, I still remember him. Therefore my heart yearns for him; I have great compassion for him.[3]

It's impossible to read this cry of God without hearing the forces of strength and tenderness in a complex and tension-filled dance. He is furious, and he disciplines his son. He can't turn against his son nor forget him, and he longs to be restored and at peace with his rebellious child.

There is a running theological debate about this conflict and whether to deny, ignore, or accept it. One school of thought maintains that God is one, and therefore he is not divided. He is serene, at perfect peace, and feels no internal conflict. Aristotle conceived of god as the "unmoved mover." Likewise, many theologians from Aquinas to Calvin assumed that God had no affective side comparable to human emotions and that all the biblical statements about the conflict between God's strength and his mercy were purely anthropomorphic—intended only to communicate in simplified language that which couldn't fully impart ultimate truth.

This is an example of rising to God's defense when he doesn't need to be defended. Far too often theology is an effort to take the embarrassment away from a God who makes the mistake of revealing himself as too profoundly "human"—at times far more human than the theologians who labor to strip him of his rather odd, idiosyncratic personality.

God wrestles with himself regarding his relationship to his sinful children. It follows, then, that God struggles to parent his rebellious kids. As much as we despair over our children's misbehavior and stubbornness, we can never presume that our own struggle is on a par with the internal conflict God feels over us. To comprehend the utter wonder and mystery of this divine conflict is to be freed as a parent not only to struggle, but to fail—and to fail without losing hope. We are to reveal God's character even as we fail as parents. That's part of what it takes to reflect both God's strength and his mercy.

God's Calling on Our Lives

God calls us to image him as we walk the earth. If this calling seems absolutely ridiculous, we also should realize that it's completely unavoidable. Since we're made in the image of God, it is built into who we are. Short of our predisposition to sin, we reflect, mirror, or reveal something about God in every aspect of our being. We are built to make new paths and new babies. We are wired to build towers and nurture a dying aunt in a nursing home. We are called to strength—a creative force that shapes the world. We are called to tenderness—a relational genesis that creates, nourishes, and directs relationships toward the glory of God.

If strength and tenderness, creativity and relationship, comprise our calling, then bearing the image of God must reveal the core directives for parenting. We are wired to call our children to subdue and rule, to fill and multiply.[4]

SUBDUING AND RULING

The notion of subduing is to trod down a path in a virgin forest. It means to put our mark on something by naming a vision, a process, or a product and then taking a risk to create it. Ruling is to oversee the creation in order to protect it and then grow it to new and even more superlative glory.

I recall the day when my son, who was three at the time, sat in our library with me. He was unusually quiet. I should have known something was amiss, but I was engrossed in my book and, as usual, I was writing notes in the margins. My son sat across from me, a red crayon in his hand. He too was reading and writing. His face was deadly serious about the task of subduing the book as he marked each page and then proceeded to the next. I gasped when I saw his crime. He looked at me as though I were crazy. He was doing the same thing his father was: subduing and ruling.

Much of what we parents call mischievous or bratty behavior is really our children's coloring outside the lines to see where a new path may take them. Children are meant to explore and trod down. They are meant to spill milk and track in dirt. They are also meant to push boundaries into complexities they can't imagine, until they are in over their head.

Years ago when my family went skiing, I typically decided what slopes we would traverse. My children always wanted to take the steepest slope possible. I rarely gave in to their requests, but it soon became clear that my caution was due to my own desire to avoid danger. As the kids improved, however, we began to take harder slopes. They always wanted to up the ante to the next hardest run. My task as a parent was to wisely choose the parameters of danger and risk that I believed were within their range—and just slightly beyond. After a few years, I realized that my children had exceeded my level of skiing expertise. It was then time to let them choose steeper slopes on their own and ski without my direct supervision.

If we refuse to give our children the opportunity to press limits, they'll take the risks anyway, but often in silence or deceit. Such hidden risks will never be shared, processed, and enjoyed. There will be no mutual learning, no opportunity for parent and child to teach each other about what it means to subdue and rule.

Subduing and ruling always takes us into danger. And a child who is kept from danger will never learn to be bold, free, and brave. As parents, we know that today's world requires that our children be all three. But in addition to subduing and ruling, our children are also meant to fill the earth.

FILLING AND MULTIPLYING

The most literal work of filling and multiplying is done when we make love, conceive, and bring forth a child. But that's just a beginning. The process of lovemaking, growing the seed and egg, and birthing requires face-to-face, heart-to-heart, body-to-body intimacy. As such, the divine commission to fill and multiply becomes far more than sexual union and childbirth. It is engaging in relationship with another to grow glory.

Two friends who meet for lunch to catch up and suffer and rejoice together are filling the earth with a fragrance of life and multiplying the glory of God.

On the other hand, two friends who meet to gossip about a third fill the earth with a noxious odor and multiply division and heartache. We are constantly going about the task of subduing and ruling and filling and multiplying, though not always for God's glory.

At age nine, my son Andrew was an accomplished skier and snowboarder. He loved to take friends from outside our home state of Colorado on the ski slopes. He superintended them well and chose slopes appropriate for their ability level. After a number of such adventures, we allowed him to take friends of any age anywhere on the slopes.

Now Andrew has a cousin and fellow snowboarder, John, whom he is wickedly serious about trying to impress. During their first time on the slopes together, Andrew was glorying in the pleasure of cutting a path in new snow. He chose a slope that was far above both boys' ability. They made it down alive, but not without undue risk and terror. It was definitely an experience in subduing and ruling—but it was far more than that.

As Andrew attempted to snowboard terrain no one had ever traversed, he was trying to impress his cousin. Such an attempt to gain respect from another person falls into the category of filling. To conquer a new world with a comrade (subduing) is a form of filling and multiplying relationship because, in this case, the experience bonded the two boys with stories that will likely last a lifetime. It was an unwise decision, but almost all subduing and filling requires a risk that later may appear foolhardy. God calls us to venture and risk when he calls us into unknown terrain.

And when God calls us, his strength demands that we obey him. That is one way he ensures our welfare, and it is a primary way that he brings order to our world. But from our vantage point, the process seems like something other than obedience. Parents naturally seek their children's safety, and for many parents that means avoiding risk. But our children are moving toward obedience when they take on a black diamond ski slope in order to impress their cousin. My son was unwise in his choice, but he was following God's calling as he took a huge risk and as he desired to gain his cousin's respect. If he refused to either desire respect or take a risk, then he would be disobedient to the way God has wired him. Remember that our commission as bearers of God's image is to subdue and fill the earth.

Separate But Together

Just as God's character is expressed in the polarities of strength and mercy, so he calls us to another set of opposing forces: individuation and intimacy. We obey God when we seek to distinguish our individual self as unique and unlike anyone else (individuation). We also obey him when we give ourselves to others for their good (intimacy). Individuation requires us to experience each moment as a choice to be the person God made us to be. Intimacy requires us to choose to yield our individuality in order to join another in becoming something greater than our individual being.

If you play a team sport, you know the necessity of this process. You may be built lean and fast or thick and strong. If you are lean and fast, you will likely become a wide receiver; if you are thick and strong, a lineman. In each case, you must learn and suffer as a unique individual to become the best you can be. You must individuate to perform well in your position. However, no matter how good you become, you must submit your individuality to the team. If you are a great center but your team needs a defensive lineman, then you must turn from what you have become to be something other for the good of the community.

In the same way, an excellent musician may prefer to play the cello, but her unique gifts enable her to play first violin. What is the wisest and best decision? Choose to be unique and yourself, or choose to give away your first choice in order to serve someone or something greater than yourself? Obedience to God will never allow us to escape the tension of his demand that we be both uniquely ourselves and also intimately involved with others. Sadly, many choose one side over the other or one element of obedience to God rather than both. That is one of the flawed choices that leads us to hiding and blaming.

In case you haven't noticed, obeying God gets us into more trouble than we would like. It certainly gets our children in trouble. After all, obedience is far more than following clear rules. And there are very few direct, unequivocal commands in the Bible (ten of them immediately come to mind). Instead, in the teaching of Jesus, we are called to love one another from the heart and be guided by God's Spirit instead of the flesh. These commands establish limits that we need in our pursuit of obedience. But seldom do they tell us exactly what to do. Do I go out for a Saturday-morning breakfast to read the paper, slow the week down, and drink in a sip of silence? Or should I rise before my family, clean the garage, mow the lawn, and wash the dog before other commitments interfere? These are two radically different options, and either choice could involve obedience or rebellion. The difference can be understood in the context of blaming and hiding. Rebellion against God is usually a refusal to individuate by hiding, and it's a refusal to be intimate by blaming.

HIDING

The dynamics of blaming and hiding are played out in the creation account. Adam and Eve chose to flee from God, so they hid behind a bush. They were naked, and they refused to stand before God and confess their rebellion. Instead they heeded the cry of shame and fled his presence.[5] Hiding is a refusal to own up to who we are, where we are, and what we have done. It's a flight from the consequences of accountability and responsibility, the products of individuation.

To individuate we must name what is true and then accept the gifts or consequences arising from our actions. For example, my older daughter was accepted at all eight colleges to which she applied, and seven gave her financial assistance. But none gave her enough to cover all her bills beyond the money we could afford to chip in. In each case Annie would either have to take out a loan or get a job during the school year in addition to a summer job.

Annie needed to make a decision, but she procrastinated and wavered. I asked her: "Is it that you don't know where you really want to go, or is it that you don't want to work during the year or bear the financial responsibility of a loan?" My question helped her get closer to the real issue, but she still tried to put off her decision. She was hiding.

It is far easier to avoid knowing what we want or where we need to go than it is to make a choice. It's natural to want to bury our head in the sand when life-determining decisions are required. Do I marry this guy? Do I go on to graduate school? Do I follow my passion and become an artist or opt for a "sensible" career in business?

Who knows? But I know exactly when I am hiding from a project, a phone call, a moment of conflict, or a decision. And each time I hide from God's calling to subdue and rule, I am far more disobedient than if I take action and make the wrong decision. Our children share the human propensity to hide, so it's the task of every parent to make it difficult, or nearly impossible, for them to rebel against God by hiding. We are called to ask them time and again, "Where are you, Son? Where are you, Daughter?" We must call our children to choose, even knowing that their choices may be crummy. Oddly, the more we call our children to choose rather than to hide, the more *we* must choose, and the less foliage there will be for us to hide behind.

God in all his wildness reveals himself to us when we move, even when we blunder and choose unwisely, rather than when we sit passively waiting for the right answer to show itself. The more we are obedient to subdue and fill, with eyes and heart open to him, the more he will guide and reveal his excruciating passion for us. But hiding is only one of the problems involved in rebellion. The other is our readiness to assign blame.

BLAMING

Adam and Eve, once exposed, chose to turn their rage against God and each other. Adam blamed God for creating Eve and then blamed her for giving him the fruit. Eve turned her guns against the snake.[6] Both found it easier to attack someone else rather than to cry out for God's mercy. When we've been damaged or we've harmed another person, it is nearly impossible to ask for help and care. Instead, blaming another person enables us to cut off the shame that has been exposed and then destroy the one who has exposed us.

Blaming gives a false sense of power to the person who feels naked and weak. That person settles for independence by denying the desire for restoration and intimacy. Blaming also numbs any desire to obtain mercy and tenderness. Think how often when you feel hurt, it is easier to turn cold and angry. To be hurt and then desire to feel someone's tender care feels like a double wound. We prefer a quicker deadening of the hurt by turning to anger. At least that's how it seems. But instead of deadening the pain, we simply escalate the tension and hatred, and both parties intensify the pattern of hiding and blaming.

Blaming is always a refusal to be needy and dependent on the other person who might rightfully turn against us for our failure. It's a fight against the allure of intimacy. And at times, the blaming is not directed against another person, but toward our self. Adam and Eve turned against God and each other, but eventually their sorrow was turned against themselves. It is only human to blame oneself.

Blaming oneself is no less an effort to escape the need for intimacy. If I attack myself as stupid or ugly or undesirable, then I cut myself off from both the desire and the need to invest myself in others. Self-blame invalidates the legitimacy of my hunger for love and the even greater desire to offer love to another. The result is usually a loss of both individuation and intimacy. To be intimate we must be open and humble before another person and allow that person to "name" us. To be named by a child is to be humble enough to hear both his accusations and his desires. We will be called to change, to sacrifice some independence to the welfare of another. That is intimacy, and it grows from our hunger for relationship. Only by living in the tension of individuation and intimacy rather than hiding and blaming can we discover what it means to be the parents God calls us to be.

In fact, it is in this process that we begin to reflect God's character into the lives of our children. As we choose to live in the grace of God's freedom, we invite our children to be free. As we express our need for forgiveness, we reveal the heart of our Father who forgives. As we celebrate, humbly and passionately, the wonder of forgiveness, we picture for our children what it means to be received back into the arms of God. We are a living Sunday-school lesson every day as we interact with our children within the character of God.

The Redemption of God

Attempting to reflect the character of God is a win-win proposition. No one can do it well on a consistent basis, but we are blessed when we fail because it is in our failure that we discover and are embraced most radically by God's character. If we truly believed this, we would be much less likely to hide.

Hiding intensifies fear. We run and hide because we are afraid, and then as we crouch behind a bush, hoping not to be found, our heart beats with terror at being discovered. The sound of God's approaching footsteps tells us that he is near and our ruse is about to be exposed. It's inevitable that we will be found by the omniscient God of the universe.

To be exposed is to be seen as naked and impotent. Impotence makes us aware that we lack the strength to subdue our world as we desire. But we need to know that we are impotent because none of us will learn what it truly means to be strong and bold unless we have been broken and shattered. Whenever strength is exercised apart from a deep taste of impotence, it is controlling and shaming. Without an awareness of our deep impotence, we are full of self-satisfaction and arrogance. But strength that has been tempered by failure will be generous and tender, nourishing and kind.

Jesus chose to experience impotence in order to free us to live out God's character. "But Christ has rescued us from the curse pronounced by the law," wrote the apostle Paul. "When he was hung on the cross, he took upon himself the curse for our wrongdoing."[7]

Jesus endured mockery of his impotence. A sign was hung over his head that identified him as, in essence, "The king of the Jews who can't save himself." He suffered absolute emptiness and loneliness as he cried out, "My God, my God, why have you forsaken me?"[8] His willingness to bear the curse of failure and loneliness guarantees his promise that we never need fear that we will be equally exposed and alone before the fierce and unrelenting eyes of God. Jesus faced the fullness of the Father's wrath so that we will never know God's strength turned against us. And Jesus faced the fullness of his Father's abandonment so that we will never be alone or forsaken.

In my failure to live out God's character, I come face to face with the awful and awesome strength and tenderness of God. In that encounter, I am invited to embrace his love in order to offer that love to my children. If we are to learn God's character in the midst of failure, how much more so are our children?

Rightly understood, this way of handling our failures is a model of enormous importance. Children learn about the character of God when they sin and are then mishandled by their parents. When parents sin against their children's sin, there is hope that the mess of sin compounding sin will turn all eyes to the only One who can love us perfectly. In other words, when parents allow sin to expose sin as well as the far deeper reality of grace, God's character begins to provide the framework of safety and freedom.

Does this mean I should sin so that my children will better understand the gospel? Not deliberately, but we don't have to try hard to sin. It's abundant even when we're trying our best to avoid it. All we need to do is be willing to allow our sin and failures to become part of the discussion of what it means to parent well—and part of the process of opening our children's eyes to God's grace and mercy.

The dilemma is simple. It is far easier to cling to one side or the other of God's character—either to his strength or to his mercy. So we offer our children strength without tenderness and find a rigidly secure world founded on religious certainty. Or we go the other way, offer them tenderness without strength, and live in the loosely nurturing world of the hypertolerant. Both extremes pervert God's character. He is both/and, not either/or.

Meeting Our Children in the Middle of God

A parent has only one core task: to reveal God. And the paradox is that in the certainty of failure, we are most able to reveal God's character. To fail and then to reveal God—and to do this well—we must live a life that is *both* strong and tender. We must refuse to grant our allegiance to the popular and false polarity. We must reject the black-and-white, fill-in-the-blanks approach to life.

The most common black-and-white approach assumes that following the correct rules guarantees the desired results. Our children will turn out well if we take them to Sunday school, have regular family devotions, pray for them, and support the right religious and political causes. The same tunnel-vision mentality can be found, with an utterly different surface structure, in a family that is consumed with bolstering the children's self-esteem, musical skills, sports prowess, and stage presence. The family of the conservative right assumes that an adherence to correct doctrine and public values will win the day. The family of the liberal left presumes that good genes, coaching, and performance will win the day. Both families rely on external measures of success, and both are equally wrong.

Parents of either stripe believe that they will produce the right kind of children by practicing the right method. This is a rote, color-by-numbers view of parenting, and it fails to reflect both real life and the character of

God. The biblical pattern for parenting is strewn with mystery, paradox, failure, redemption, and reconciliation—it is always both/and, never either/or. Meeting our children in the middle of God means we are willing to be thrown about by the wild, woolly depths of his character. And swimming in the belly of God's character requires us to know that the moment we put our feet on his strength, we will land on his tenderness—and of course the reverse is equally true. Consider now the results if we reject the mystery of God's both/and character in favor of rote, fill-in-the-blanks parenting.

THE ERROR OF DOING RIGHT OVER BEING RIGHT

Not long ago on a commercial airline flight, I sat with the twenty-something daughter of a prominent Christian leader. After a brief period of conversation, I thought I would lose my mind. She was arrogant, totally full of herself and her family's wisdom. I think highly of her family, and if I am to be judged by my children—or my children by me—then I, too, am hopeless. But I couldn't help noticing that this young woman had no interest in anything outside her own world. She refused to ask my wife a single question about our family. She failed to ask me a single question about the graduate school we have begun or how my wife and I met or anything else that would create conversation interplay.

However, when I suggested that many Christians are frightfully narrow in their encounter with a fallen culture, I was lectured on the necessity of providing even adult children with clear limits in order to protect them from the godless culture of "movies, magazines, and music." I felt as if I were listening to a telephone solicitor. Any attempt to get this woman off her stock sales pitch was met with firm insistence that I return to "the truth." There was no room for debate. She knew the answers and insisted that I accept them.

The either/or worldview of the conservative right presumes that there is a clear and unambiguous list of things to believe and do that will ensure the desired outcome. With parents having such easy access to this proven formula, though, why aren't more kids turning out right? I have my theories, and here is one of them: This either/or system defines righteousness as right-doing in contrast with doing things from the core of right-being.

When we define righteousness as right-doing, it's too easy to skew the standard of what is right. We often confuse biblically warranted doing with the accepted, North American, middle-class orientation to life. In other words, kids are on track if they are headed toward solid citizenship as college-educated or trade-school-trained, gainfully employed, patriotic individuals. This approach to parenting may contribute to the stability of our society and the health of the nation's economy, but it doesn't promote a view of the gospel as foolishness.[9] Instead it substitutes respectability and conformity for the mystery of God's righteousness that has become ours only by the death and resurrection of Jesus Christ.

This right-doing approach to God and his righteousness views the Bible as a manual for living life rather than as a text that invites the human heart into a wild and strange encounter with God. It makes Christian faith a curriculum to be studied rather than the pursuit of a relationship with our untamed God. The instruction-manual approach to the Bible seeks safety and stability, although God promises us nothing beyond his presence. The blessings of life are given to us by God according to his will and purposes, and not based on our faithfulness in following the rules.

Lest you think I'm grinding an ax against the conservative right, let me assure you that the liberal left is guilty of an equally damaging error.

THE ERROR OF SELF-ESTEEM IN PLACE OF RIGHTEOUSNESS

I sat with the late twenty-something child of a major leader in the recovery movement. She has grown up with a profound awareness of the destructiveness of shame, intolerance, and dogmatism. I asked her what parameters her parents had provided in childhood to help her discern the difference between right and wrong. "Right is giving a person the opportunity to be free," she answered. "Wrong is limiting creativity and choice."

I pressed her and asked, "But at times when you were growing up, weren't there rules and boundaries that required your parents to step in and make you miserable?"

She thought for a moment. "Mom was really involved in getting her doctorate, and my dad was so busy in his writing and speaking career that I was left to make most of the decisions on my own. My parents were far more concerned that I felt good about myself and seemed confident than they were about whether I should see an R-rated movie or go to a party where there might be drinking."

Many parents shove character onto the back burner in their single-minded devotion to elevating their children's self-worth and ensuring their children's mastery of social skills. These parents measure success by their children's achievements in the areas of sports, music, drama, or academics. They assume that if a child learns to succeed, the institutions that assure adult success (country clubs, Kiwanis, church, and the university alumni association) will put the finishing touches on a culturally acceptable person who serves the family, society, and God. Consequently, it's far more important to make sure one's children are coached and trained to maturity than that they are taught a view of life that is truly righteous. And while we may assume this mind-set is representative of the humanistic left, let's also admit that it's far too prevalent inside the church. What other organization is as program oriented as the American church?

I fear that this approach to God offers us a nearly irresistible incentive. It promises success as an antidote to suffering rather than godly character as a basis for serving those who are weak and poor. It views the Christian life as a series of accomplishments to be earned rather than an unpredictable, sometimes prickly, relationship to be embraced. It elevates self-esteem as the highest good and makes the experience of shame the greatest wrong, rather than leading us to embrace the shame of Jesus as the road to redemption.

Living in the Righteous Middle

If we're going to reflect the character of God into our children's lives, we need to avoid both extremes: rule-bound "righteousness" and success-obsessed social conformity. Just as God is both strong and merciful, we must take our place in the messy, impossible middle. The wise and gracious parent creates a realm of both/and and provides a framework to protect her child (in age-appropriate forms) from the ravages of undue risk and sin. Of course doing both is impossible, but it is fully required. And our inability to simultaneously provide both safety and freedom makes the gospel that much more necessary. We have to truly know forgiveness and then offer it to our children.

Safety comes from the gift of strength. I will protect my children from the bullies of the classroom and the patronizing condescension of a bad teacher. I will provide the physical skills and attitude to interact with bullies and the verbal skills and appropriate attitude for addressing a tactless or unqualified teacher. In either case, training our children to become strong must risk the violation of rules that our culture or church or neighbors consider right and righteous. But one must fail if one is to learn how to use strength in the service of righteousness.

Similarly, freedom comes from the gift of grace. Freedom is the antithesis of bondage and fearful servitude. Perfect love casts out fear and frees the heart to give and receive care, pleasure, and joy. I will not only protect my children, but I will provide them with a taste of freedom so they can play and rest. A free child can rest boldly and play restfully.

The mystery of God's calling to parents is great. The more children know safety, the stronger they can become. The more they know tenderness, the freer they can be. And greater strength yields more tenderness; greater tenderness produces a fierce commitment to the weak and the needy. Oddly, when God's strength and mercy are woven together over time, children learn to live in the middle of the mystery of God.

Learning Strength and Mercy

We had only been living in Puget Sound for two weeks when my daughter Amanda stood near my desk and waited for me to sense her presence. When I turned, her face was sad and resolute. She said, "I've caused trouble for you. I'm sorry, and then again I'm not. I need to tell you something." I was all ears.

Amanda was twelve. Her features were those of a girl, but I could tell that whatever she was going to tell me involved a major transition from being a little girl to a new level. She said, "I hit the boy across the street, and his father is angry and wants to talk with you."

I was utterly stunned. Amanda is not a pugilist. I asked for the context, and she told me this story. The second day we lived in our new home, my son Andrew (then age eight) had been beaten up by several boys in the neighborhood. I hadn't heard a word about this. Amanda said he was too embarrassed to tell me. She told the twelve-year-old neighbor boy to pick on someone his own size and that, if he bothered Andrew again, he would pay. That day the neighbor boy beat Andrew up again. Amanda found her brother crying and discovered the cause. She walked over to the neighbor's house, rang the doorbell, and decked the boy when he answered the door.

She came and told me. I was horrified; I was proud. I'd rather have a child who makes mistakes than one who chooses to hide from the conflict and heartache of this world. She should have come to me first. Andrew ought to have told me of his struggle. For whatever reason, though, they had chosen to take matters into their own hands.

Amanda had chosen to subdue and rule. She did well. She failed. Both are true. She then turned herself in to face the consequences and to name what was true. It killed me to punish her, but I did. We went across the street and talked to the neighbor. I later sat with the family and tried to work out a plan that didn't involve any more violence. Amanda couldn't go out with friends that evening, and she was required to watch a half-hour of World Wrestling Federation drama.

God has called us to the impossible task of parenting. But this same task is impossibly wonderful. To take sin seriously is to always see it in light of the calling of what our children are to become and what we are to be. We (and they) are to rule and subdue, to multiply and fill. They (and we) are to be both strong and tender, as imitators of God.

No matter how paradoxical it is, this mystery is God's intention and calling for us.

CHAPTER 8

The Perseverance of Hope

Dreaming God's Desires for Our Children

We have seen that God's calling for parents is a humanly impossible task. As hard as we try not to, we stumble and fail. Then we get up and stumble again. While our repeated failure may grieve us, it's actually the path that invites God to become all we could ever want him to be. It is when sin abounds that grace grows even greater.

But grace is a problematic concept for parents: We don't truly believe in it. If we did, we'd relax and invite our children to risk and fail, play and fall. We'd know far less turmoil when they got a bad grade or wrestled with relational ups and downs. We'd trust that, even in the middle of the struggles, a greater good was growing if we only had eyes to see.

At heartbreaking moments and even in the daily ordering of life, we question the efficacy of God's grace, and yet we believe in luck and hard work and the power of our social organizations to do good for our kids through child-centered activities. Our reliance on everything but grace has us exhausted, worried, and secretly counting the days until our little cherubs are out of their diapers, or in school, or out of adolescence, or out of the house.

The desire to rush through one stage to get to the next is the idiocy of believing that the grass really is greener on the other side. It isn't, of course. Don't rush the future; generally parenting only gets harder.

I was talking with a friend about his youngest son, and he said, "Well, I've got five more years until he's eighteen. We can make it that long, I suppose, but it seems like an eternity." His son is a fairly typical teen who drives his parents batty. And the father is handling the pain of the present by counting the days to having an empty nest free of chaos, noise, and demands. When he said it would be five years, I knew exactly what he meant because I said to myself, "We have four years, three months, and eleven days until that glorious moment when all three kids are gone, we've sold the house, moved onto a boat, and can only be accessed through e-mail." I am a fool.

What ran through my mind next was a conversation I'd had with a father whose son is in his early forties. This sixty-something dad said, "You never really stop caring, nor do you ever really forget the past, because you wish you had the opportunity to do things differently." His son was caught up in the dotcom economy and had invested years of labor and most of his savings in the allure of fast money. When tech stocks crashed, so did this man's son. He was out of work, depressed, and on the brink of ruin. The father had loaned his son money, and the result was even greater distance and a steeper depression. The father looked at me and said, "Tell your readers, 'Once a parent, always a parent.' Parenting is for life."

We are never to stop living in the middle of God's strength and his mercy. We are never to stop answering our children's two core questions: "Am I loved?" and "Can I get my own way?" We are meant to persevere in parenting through the sorrow and the shame. There really is no other way.

Sorrow and Shame

A foolish child brings grief to a father and bitterness
a mother.[1]

The father of godly children has cause for joy. What a pleasure it is to have wise children. So give your parents joy! May she who gave you birth be happy.[2]

My child, how happy I will be if you turn out to be wise! Then I will be able to answer my critics.[3]

A proverb is a wise saying. It summarizes life in a pithy, poignant fashion. Every culture formulates proverbs to cut to the quick of complex matters. We say, "Women [or men]—can't live with them; can't live without them." A proverb can be as simple as "Why ask why?" It's a slam-in-your-mouth thought that exposes the truth and then instructs you in a manner of living.

The Old Testament book of Proverbs is filled with wise sayings about raising children. Perhaps one of the most painful is a reminder to both the child and the parent of the shame that can come through a child.[4]

Children exercise their greatest power in their inherent ability to break their parent's hearts. The weakness of parents is the reality that they can mold, but they can't make a child. The only making a parent can do is at conception; all other parental influence is shaped by this odd reversal of power. Parents are big, and children are small. And children are for years utterly dependent on their parents. However, at a precocious age, children realize that they are free and the parents are bound.

That moment came for my daughter Annie when she was sixteen months old. She was walking with confidence and, like many firstborns, had developed language at a frightening rate. She was standing with one hand on the refrigerator door, and I was sitting on a stool at the kitchen counter. She alternately looked at me and then stared at the door. I soon noticed her point of interest. It was a piece of rubber molding at the bottom of the door that had begun to come out of its track.

Annie knelt down and began to pull on the rubber edge. I said, "No, Annie. Don't pull. No, no." She looked me square in the face. Her eyes were unafraid and unmoved. She clearly understood the prohibition. She turned back and began to pull on the edge. I said it again, "Annie, no. If you continue, I will have to discipline you." She looked at me again and said, "No spanking, Daddy." I smiled and replied, "Annie, if you pull on it again, you will be spanked." She looked at me, looked at the compelling rubber edge that beckoned, looked back at me, and then turned resolutely to the piece of rubber, put both hands on the edge, and pulled as hard as her little body could.

She didn't merely defy me. She did so with complete awareness of the consequences for disobeying and then said in her little sixteen-month-old soul, *I don't give a rip! It feels good, I want to do it, and the cost of a spanking is not as great as the pleasure of seeing what this rubber molding feels like in my hands when I yank.* She weighed the cost-benefit ratio and went for it. I was stunned. I likely spanked her, she probably cried, and we both went toddling on into our day. What stuck for me was that even the promise of pain had no ultimate power to convince my daughter—or any of my children—to not do what they really wanted to do.

Our children are not extensions of ourselves; they are separate, autonomous beings. They are free to choose their own way in spite of pain and consequences. Even at sixteen months, Annie was free to bring me sorrow and shame. A child is free, and the parent is bound. The parent is a slave to love; a child must break those bonds to become a new being.

The Gift of Sorrow

There are gifts every child brings a parent, but one of the strangest is heartache. The heart is literally a huge muscle that pumps life through the extremities of our being. Just like any other muscle, it must be exercised to grow stronger, and that discipline requires some sweat and pain. So does the growth of our emotional heart. Our love grows to the degree that we suffer and refuse to turn cold and hard.

In a world like ours, suffering is not a choice, but misery is. If in the face of suffering we say, "Enough, no more. I quit," we are choosing misery, not growth. To be a parent is to suffer. The suffering is related to God's calling on our lives to allow our children to hurt, to fail, and to suffer consequences. The suffering is also personal because we will fail as parents by not being enough and also by being too much.

Sorrowing Their Hurt

I recall a phrase my wife, Becky, used as if she uttered it only minutes ago. It came when one of our children had hit the floor hard and loud. I was indisposed and could not see the scene, but it was obvious from the sounds that tears were rolling down our daughter's cheeks. And the longer no adult responded, the more intense the raging flow became. Eventually my wife said, "Don't bleed on the carpet, and if we need to take you to the hospital, let me know." I wanted to laugh and scream. Our child was wailing, and my wife was nonchalant. I couldn't believe her lack of care!

When I finally saw Becky's face, though, I realized that she was strikingly sad and that her calm was more a choice than a reflection of ease. She had chosen to honor our child with the dignity of suffering rather than showering her with overweening parental protection. My wife sorrowed and resisted the natural urge to scoop up her child and take away the pain.

Every parent has watched a child suffer but could not—or should not—stop the pain. I will never forget the wilting, piercing, confused eyes of my son as a physician stuck a needle in his head to numb the skin before sewing up his wound. His eyes said, "Daddy, don't let this man hurt me!" No manner of explanation or assurance could take away his sense of betrayal. I watched my son hurt and his eyes turn from mine in anger. I would gladly have taken the stitches tenfold and without Novocaine if that would have alleviated his pain and his confusion.

A day doesn't go by that I am not a witness to my children's suffering. The two little girls who teased my daughter for wearing new tennis shoes were almost accosted on the street. The only thing that stopped me was a clear mental image of the newspaper headline: PSYCHOLOGIST ATTACKS TWO SMALL CHILDREN FOR SHAMING HIS DAUGHTER. The hurts of life—physical, relational, emotional—are utterly intolerable when I see one of my kids suffer, or when I must be the one who allows or even at times brings that suffering into their lives.

Sorrow reveals that something is out of whack in the world. It further exposes that I am mostly powerless to stop the hurt. Nothing like watching a child suffer brings on the salty taste of tears and blood.

SORROWING THEIR FAILURE

We desperately want our children to succeed. Otherwise it makes no sense that we push them into the same type of exhausting, overscheduled lives that we struggle with ourselves. We live in an age of success obsession and failure phobia. Still, failure is the wisest teacher and the deepest motivator for gaining a greater grasp of what we need to do to achieve our desires. Without failure we would not only be bored, but we would never learn to love learning.

But tell that to a child who is the worst—the absolute worst—on the gymnastics mat. I recall the horror of watching all the other eight-year-olds bounding onto the mat, turning somersaults, and following the barking commands of the Eastern-bloc coach—all except my daughter Annie. She was tentative, awkward, and self-conscious. I watched for a half-hour and couldn't stand her discomfort, so I headed for the parking lot.

My hands were shaking as I stood outside, trying to generate enough energy to power the little-train-that-could standing inside on the mat. I knew she could, I knew she could, or at least I *thought* she would, but she didn't, and I couldn't figure out what to do. Oddly, all our children's failures are ours as well. In fact, they often are more ours than theirs.

When Annie came out to the car, she looked at me and said, "I stink. That was awful, and I don't want to ever do that again." I agreed, but clearly I had suffered more than she did. I still have nightmares about that afternoon.

A child must be allowed to experiment, and experimentation requires falling flat on your face. Parents obviously shouldn't let a small child play in traffic. Some experimentation is deadly and wrong; other experimentation is age-dependent and to be moderated by parental involvement. Nevertheless, when a child smacks her face on the floor, there is a clutch in the parent's stomach, a tensing of the hands, and an involuntary, hair-trigger instinct to swoop down and rescue her from the frustration and shame. In this case instinct is often wrong. Parents need to let a child learn the lessons that come only by failing.

Sorrowing Their Consequences

The classic parental self-delusion "This will hurt me more than you" is not a complete lie. There are a few spankings that did hurt my hand more than they troubled my child's rear end. Far more often, though, consequences have come to my children's lives due to their failures that have been as hard on me, if not harder, than the fallout for them.

One of the most recent was a State of Washington history project that utterly ruined two weekends for our family. My seventh-grade son was assigned the task of investigating an odd little San Juan Islands boundary dispute known as The Pig War. No worry that you have never heard of this conflict in the annals of American history. There is precious little data available. In fact, the conflict involved the death of a British pig that was shot by an American settler and stirred two great nations to muster troops to defend their claims to the same island territory. No shot was fired and no death occurred, save the poor pig. You already know about as much as is known about the dispute and far more than you ever cared to know.

I know what I do about The Pig War only because my son left a huge project—including maps, interviews, and video production—to the last moment. He had "forgotten" about the due date, and anyway he figured it would only take an hour or two. What complicated the scenario was a dialogue my wife and I had had a few days earlier about the need for me to be more involved in our children's schoolwork. I had agreed, figuring it meant a few minutes every now and then to check their homework. I hadn't planned on descending into the arcane minutiae of a bloodless (save for the pig) war. And all of that paled in light of the frustrations ahead in videotaping, downloading data to a satanic computer, and then editing, adding music, headings, and fades in and out—all of which brought me within inches of committing a violent act.

Instead of exploding, however, I took a deep breath and wisely grounded my son for the remainder of his adolescence. But providing discipline is not all that easy for anyone. It is a simple fact that when a parent grounds a child, he also grinds all of life to a halt. When a parent says, "If you don't change your attitude, then we won't be going to the movie," the result is a loss of the movie, a breaking of the parent-child pleasure bond, and the emotional weight for the parent that comes with being the heavy. No wonder it's easier to rescue a child or ignore his behavior. We don't want the child to suffer, and we don't want to suffer his suffering and ours combined. But an undisciplined child—or one that is enabled to escape the consequences of his actions—is truly an unloved child.

It may seem gracious and kind to ignore troubling, childish behavior. But dismissing such behavior injures the child by insulating him from suffering and failing. The result for the child is a loss of the confidence that comes from surmounting obstacles, including the ones inside us that foil much of what we want to do. An undisciplined child fails to grow in respect for himself and others. A parent must bring consequences that fit the offense that, if left unaddressed, would hinder a child's development. Those moments will be filled with reluctance, doubt, and sorrow for the parent.

As often as we must limit our children's movement, we are called on the other hand to suffer their freedom. Sometimes that involves watching them make decisions that we know or suspect will lead to failure and unpleasant consequences. Other times it means insisting that they make a decision on their own when they would prefer to give that responsibility to us. When do we step in and limit their suffering? When do we help them avoid failure? When do we remit the consequences and offer grace, and when do we stick to the letter of the law? Some decisions are as clear as life and death, and others are as murky as life itself. In most cases an expert or another parent will tell you unequivocally that it would have been far wiser to have done the exact opposite of what you chose to do. Parenting is an invitation to suffering because no one really knows what to do.

Perhaps the greatest task of parenting is humbly staying involved even when we don't have a clue what to do. It's the task of a good parent to face the truth that no parent is good enough. No parent is sufficient to provide for her children what only grace can offer. It is the calling of every parent to be deeply, fervently aware of his or her need for grace.

Accounting for Our Own Failure

If parenting were only about our kids, we would suffer far less. Parenting ought to be mostly about our children, but more often than not, it's too much about us. We fail and bring sorrow to our children, which then returns to us with tragic dividends. Our failures can be summarized in three categories: unthinking, reactive, and mean.

OUR UNTHINKING FAILURE

My daughter took a terrible fall on the ski slope ahead of me, and I skied rapidly down to her. As I went to stop, my skis came out from under me on a patch of ice, and I fell. As I slid toward her I could see panic on her face. Her fall was bad enough, but the second blow as I crashed into her was horrible. She was in tears, and I tried to comfort her; but my words couldn't take away the accident. I felt the flame of self-loathing. The words screaming inside me were far more vile than I will write, but the least of my phrases was, *You idiot, why do you think she fell in the first place? You should have known there was a patch of ice right there.*

I've left my children at school when I had promised to pick them up. I've stepped on them, dropped things on them, played too rough, and failed to deliver on promises because I simply forgot. Unthinking, insensitive, unintentional failure breaks a parent's heart.

OUR REACTIVE FAILURE

Every child learns what buttons to push to provoke a response. When their wishes aren't granted, they attempt to take a parent down with them in one last heroic gesture. My children know the exact modulation to speak with, just the proper rise of intonation that conveys their disdain for a decision I made. I usually turn up the volume. This intensifies their sense of self-righteous contempt, galvanizes my resolve, and sends us each miles away from the other. Often I will say to myself, *You're the adult. Get a grip on your anger!* But the phrase *You're the adult* only serves to fuel my anger, since the kid sitting in the car seat across from me doesn't have to pay the car insurance, house mortgage, or go to work to get the snot beat out of him every day. My child should at least appreciate the cost of making even this one car trip, let alone realize how ridiculous a request it is to stop for ice cream.

Sometimes a parent's reactive failure has nothing to do with the child. A kid is moving slowly and has not had the opportunity to survey her mom's day planner and consider the weight of her mom's responsibilities. Therefore the life-and-death command "Let's get going" only seems like a vague suggestion, not the intractable command that it truly is. Figuratively speaking, the kid is reading the sheet music for the latest song by Wilco and the parent is singing from Handel's *Messiah.* Reactive failures are suffused in self-justification, but the result is that a parent feels like a kid and the kid feels at least equal to, if not clearly superior to, the feeble parental role model.

OUR MEAN FAILURE

Let's face it—we can be mean. There are times I pick on the least of those who can do me harm. If I yell at a neighbor kid, I might have to face his parent or even the police. I might prefer to kick the dog, but the dog can bite me. At times we are angry and crazy, and our children get the brunt of our bad day, our past abuse, our parents' divorce, the loss of a job, being cut off on the freeway, and God knows what else. I can be a wreck—immature, self-centered, self-justifying, and have bad breath.

There is no cure for such harm but to confess and to ask for forgiveness. Even if we do that, which is seldom the case, it still doesn't bind up the wounds. Our request for forgiveness may keep the child from feeling crazy in the silence surrounding the failure, but it doesn't take away her hurt.

So we are left with little certainty about what to do. We often fail and then increase our children's suffering due to our lack of knowledge and wisdom. On the other hand, we often fail our children simply because we lack maturity. In either case, we suffer when our children suffer.

Parenting would be hard enough if our struggle were only with suffering. But parenting also opens our heart to experience a deeper struggle: shame. And we often become mean when our child exposes us to shame.

The Shame of Parenting

It was a terrible moment. It was my oldest daughter's first piano recital, an experience I still view as akin to hell. We sat in an audience of about ten thousand parents and had waited about four days to hear our daughter play (or so it seemed). Finally my pigtailed seven-year-old stepped onto the stage. I could barely breathe. She sat on the huge stool and began her piece. She was relaxed, and I was a wet, wrung rag. She played brilliantly until she came to the middle of the short tune, and she stopped. The audience held its collective breath. A brief moment later she began again. The audience exhaled in relief until we realized she had not progressed toward the end of her music, she had started again at the beginning.

Now we waited to see if she could plow through the middle to complete the piece. As she came to the point where she had stopped before, the audience tensed. She came to the same point, and her hands became still. The tension was thick. Annie turned to the audience and, with a little Cheshire smile, shrugged her shoulders. The audience broke into applause and laughter. The piano teacher came on stage, put the music in front of her, and she finished the piece with aplomb.

I was furious and ashamed. After the last performance of the recital, we ate the obligatory stale cookies, had some of the pink drink, and milled about congratulating children and parents. No one seemed to know what to do with my daughter or us. This only intensified my sense of being an alien, a musical idiot, and the head of an undisciplined family. My perspective was so deranged and my reaction so out of kilter that I knew there was no cure but to depart.

I signaled my wife that we had to go. She saw the tight jaw and the dark eyes and likely figured it was better if I melted down outside rather than in front of a coliseum of friends.

I walked to the car ahead of my wife and daughter. Near the car Annie grabbed my jacket and whirled me around. She said, "You hate me, don't you? Why are you so ashamed of me?"

I don't think a diagnosis of cancer handed to me on the spot would have been more frightening. I felt stripped and thrown against a wall—exposed and naked. Shame. It is a raw, soul-freezing, heart-hardening sickness. A parent is guaranteed to suffer shame, an experience which involves reversal, revelation, and some combination of rage and contempt.

I expected my daughter to perform well or at least adequately. She had reversed my expectations and desire. And all reversals throw us into discomfort. If no personal exposure results, shame will likely not occur. For example, the reversal of having a flight canceled is never due to me, so I can blame others without any direct culpability. But the moment a fault is viewed as mine, then the ingredients for shame are present. The reversal is my fault. Shame is birthed when, in the face of a personal reversal, we refuse to admit our humanity (our finiteness, frailty, and failure) and turn against ourselves with contempt.

Annie reversed my expectations and exposed our family's lack of musical prowess as well as our failure to adequately prepare our child for the performance. Then rather than accepting the beautiful timing of her shrug or the audience's warm embrace of her, I turned the reversal against her, my wife, and finally myself. I slumped into the slough of shame. Shame comes for most parents when the gift of God reverses, exposes, and intensifies the unnamed and unfinished shame in the life of the parent.

We can't help but dream for our children. Most of our initial dreams have no connection to the intelligence, aptitude, or interests of the child. Our dreams are directly and symbolically related to our own life story. In many ways, each child is a parent's blank canvas on which they can repaint their own fate.

The piano recital created a confrontation between me, the dad, and me, a fat, stupid, and unattractive kid. I was a bully who had few friends and spent a great deal of my life alone, reading, watching television, and eating Oreos. I didn't like the me of childhood, and I had promised myself that my kids would be healthy (thin), love to learn (straight-A students), and caring (popular with their peers). It's amazing how we can have reasonable and honorable dreams and goals for our children which are little more than our commitment to finally set to rights our past.

It is a fair rule: Every parent's dreams for his child must be broken in order for the child to piece together her true dreams. We can't demand that our children paint by the numbers of our already laid-out plan.

Here is the irony of our dreams: Parents must dream for their child, or the child will fail to cultivate the ground of hope. At the same time, the dreams must be breakable, or the child will live in a parental straitjacket. It is in the anguish between those two worlds where most parents will experience their dreams turning to nightmares.

Our dreams for our children may shatter, but the shards remain underfoot. Those broken parts begin to scar us and in turn send a force of contempt from us into the world. We can't live with inner mayhem without dumping that energy on those nearest to us. Shame then sears us with such heat that we turn hard in order to survive, and we turn the heat against the one who shatters our dreams. If there is an area where most parents fail to persevere, it is in dreaming for their children.

The Perseverant Dreamer

We dislike sorrow, and we utterly despise shame. For many parents, the prospect of more shattered dreams drains away the courage to dream again. It takes a profound commitment to hope if we are to find the courage we need. The apostle Paul wrote about sorrow, suffering, shame, and hope in words of enormous beauty and power. He said,

> We rejoice in the hope of the glory of God. Not only so, but we also
> rejoice in our sufferings, because we know that suffering produces perse-
> verance; perseverance, character; and character, hope. And hope does not
> disappoint us, because God has poured out his love into our hearts by the
> Holy Spirit, whom he has given us.[5]

The path to love travels through hope. And the path to hope always travels through suffering. The bridge from suffering to love, however, is built on the foundation of perseverance. If we don't endure, we won't win the race. And even if we travel at the speed of a tortoise, the perseverant racer who slogs always beats those whose fleet feet take them to rest and leisure.

Paul's words about hope invite us to travel toward the love that God has poured out for us through the Holy Spirit. The Spirit is like a fresh and wild wind that blows through us. Whether soothing our pain or tearing away our pretenses, he cries out as if a mother in hard labor with words that we can't hear but are heard by the Father and Son.[6] And each time the Spirit blows through us, our soul is aroused to hope in God. But often the dreams of a parent are at odds with the plans of the Spirit.

PARENTAL DREAMS

Our dreams for our children often are grounded on proving something about us or correcting something from our past. If my daughter can perform a piano piece flawlessly, not only are we gifted and competent, but my own past noise is drowned out in the effulgence of her glory. Our dreams are also highly acculturated. It's not likely that a financially challenged family dreams about their son getting a squash scholarship. We dream in terms that are familiar and conventional.

More often than not we dream that our children won't suffer in the same areas where we have failed. A parent who chose not to study hard and, as a result, suffered the consequences of a sloppy academic career often pushes her child to excel academically. A parent who felt adrift from the in crowd is often engrossed in securing a confident and cool demeanor for his son.

Furthermore, our dreams arise from the cultural markers that we have identified as the indicators of success. In a conservative Christian context, that might include being resolutely moral, faithful in attending youth group, knowledgeable about the Bible, and bold in proclaiming the gospel. A more socially conscious religious home might include the above dreams but would add regular volunteer work at a soup kitchen or nursing home. Each family value will be linked to the expanding dreams we have for our children.

It may be too starkly stated, but few of our dreams have to do with character, especially the character of God. We may desire or demand that our children be honest, hard-working, and polite. We may insist that they eat well, bathe at least once a day, and open the door for elderly aunts. But do we actually dream about our children becoming more tender and strong?

I don't believe the Spirit of God is too terribly concerned about whether your child or mine gets into Harvard or scores the winning goal in the state soccer championship. But the Spirit does dream about character. Do I wish to join the Spirit's dreams for my children?

DREAMS OF THE SPIRIT

The Holy Spirit constantly turns our lives toward the face of God.[7] The more we see God, the more we come to understand his calling on our life and on the lives of our children. It is our privilege to dream far bigger dreams than that good things happen and bad things don't happen to our children. We are to dream and pray and desire and speak to the possibilities that pain and tragedy and pleasure and glory will weave our children into beings who hunger to touch the face of God.

For years I prayed that my daughter Annie would be a good kid—smart, godly, happy, holy, and not the cause of too much trouble. I prayed for far more and at times far less. But I confess I seldom prayed for much other than that she would not be too hurt by life, not be harmed in an accident, and have a heart for God. And then I got a phone call in the early fall of her sophomore year in college.

Annie left to go to class one October morning. She was five minutes from her apartment when she sensed something calling her back home. She turned and went home. The bathroom door was closed and locked. She shouted to her roommate and heard nothing. She knocked and knocked, and her fear grew. Eventually she threw her body against the door, broke the lock, and found her roommate in the bathtub after having ingested six vials of pills.

The roommate was already turning blue; vomit covered her nose and mouth. Annie dragged her out of the tub, called 911, and began to administer CPR. When she called me several hours later, after enduring a horrible ambulance ride to the hospital and the cold, professional disregard of a busy hospital staff, she had aged a decade in a day.

Her words were full of agony and exhaustion: "I'm all right, Dad, but I really need you to be here as soon as you can. I really need you." I felt sick, scared, sad, furious, and oh so proud. My daughter had listened to the Spirit.

She had heard something in her own sinews that called her to act. She knows how to listen. She is able to break down doors. She knows CPR and is resourceful, passionate, and bold. She is a saver of lives.

I had dinner with a friend whom Annie had interviewed when she was working on her master's degree. The friend said to me, "Your daughter is a healer. She is gentle and comforting. She knows how to ask hard and penetrating questions, she sees things most people refuse to see, and she kindly invites you to name what is involved in the process of health. You must be very proud."

I am very, very proud. But I am less proud than humbled that the Spirit chooses to dream for Annie in a way that uses my failure and my passion and blends them into a mystery of music far more compelling than any piano recital piece.

To hope for our children is not to bind them to our dreams for their success, fame, safety, or even happiness. Neither is hope the futile effort to redeem our own past by seeing our children do better than we have done. To dream for our children is to lean into the quiet cries of the Holy Spirit that call out the true, God-given name of our child. If we refuse to quit dreaming, we may one day hear this name. We must have the hope to imagine, and the imagination to dream, the reality of God for our children.

CHAPTER 9

Naming and Being Named

How to Learn the Name God Will Give Us

Nothing is more obvious than this: Every child emerges from the womb with a different face, body, being, and mind. If this is so obvious, however, why are most parents stunned by how different their children are? Perhaps you've heard someone utter the classic line "I just don't know how these two kids can be so different when they come from the same family." What is absurdly obvious is also profoundly disconcerting due to the implications of such wild diversity. If we're so radically different even within the same family, how can anyone keep a straight face while offering us a "one size fits all" approach to parenting?

Every child is a unique tapestry, a one-time pattern never to be seen again. Considering the complexity of one person is terrifying, let alone a world populated by billions of such gloriously singular beings. And at birth each person receives a name, one name that comes to reflect the unique meaning of his or her existence.

The greatest gift we give our children is their name. We give them a last name that identifies them as part of a particular family and, for a season, becomes their safe harbor. We give them a first name and a middle name that mark them with a particular connection to their past (a grandfather, an aunt, a mentor) and/or a vision of their future. My middle child was born on my father's birthday. We named her Amanda after the southern Ohio town where my mother was born. It's a bucolic, hilly, wild place. It marked a great deal of my early childhood and adolescence, and from the moment I met Amanda I sensed she was laid back and over the edge. Her middle name is Leigh, a feminization of my father's name, Lee.

My dad loved all my children with an abandon he rarely showed to me when I was growing up. He crawled on the floor with my kids, walked them and rocked them for hours, and was a doting, picture-toting, proud grandfather. But he developed an almost otherworldly relationship with Amanda. He loved the town of Amanda and farmed the land of our family farm until he died. He treasured the land, and he adored the one who bore his name and reflected the rolling, wild hills of his heritage. It is Amanda, ten years after my father's death, who will tear up when we speak his name.

Names are the most powerful syllables we speak and the most dear sounds we hear. Nothing is more important than the gift of the name we give and the name the child discovers for herself. It is this odd, terribly difficult, and wonderful process that makes naming a lifelong process. We are given a name without having a say in the matter. And while we spend a lifetime understanding our earthly name, we also discover the hints of a new name that will be given to us by God.[1]

If that is not odd enough, the parent will come to know his or her own name through the experience of the children learning their name and glimpsing the contours of the name that is to come. In my children's discovery of their true name, I too find something of the geography of meaning that helps me hear and discover the name that will one day be mine. I may name my child, but my child comes to name me as well. This is another way that children raise parents.

The Uniqueness of Names

If God were being named today, based on our experience and understanding of how he continually reveals his character, he might bear the name Strength and Mercy.[2] That is one name, not two, because these attributes come as one. God is not Strength on odd days and Mercy on even days. He is both at all times.

God invites us parents to participate in an eternal process of giving and receiving a taste of his strength and mercy. As we have seen, we are called to reflect God's character into the lives of our children, and we can't do that without this paired combination.

As parents we are to name our children and be named by them. I recall the day my son named my younger daughter. Amanda was five when Andrew was just starting to talk. He called me "Da." Becky, as "Mama," was the only multisyllabic being in the universe. Annie was "An," and for some reason, in Andrew's world, Amanda didn't have a name. I recall him sitting in his high-chair at breakfast and looking at Amanda like he saw her for the first time, and he said, "Day." He pointed at her and said again and again, "Day, Day, Day." His face was full of delight, and I looked at Amanda. There were tears in her eyes, and she had a look of utter awe. The one who names is strong; the one who is named is full of awe and gratitude. To give a name is a gift; to receive a gift is to be full of tender joy.

I was named after a dog. My grandfather, Oliver Wendell Holmes Bope, told my mother in no uncertain terms not to name his first grandson with any of the names he had been saddled with. He told her, if she wanted to honor him, to name his first grandson after his favorite dog. My grandfather was an earthy, vulgar prince of a man who was unwilling to give a fool the ground to stand on and was a ferocious champion of the rights of animals, the weak, and the poor. He ran a group of pointers that were from the Comanche line, and his favorite of that line was named Dan. The dog's name was not Daniel; nor is mine. My name is simply Dan. I am grateful to this day that my mother didn't name me Comanche.

It is my heritage to be named after a dog. But its meaning far exceeds that of being a hunter with a good nose. In Hebrew, Daniel means the "justice of God." I have no idea if my grandfather knew this ancient meaning of the word, or if the word found him and impressed itself on him. But I am a hunter—a therapist and a man called to name the injustice of abuse. How did that come about? How do any of us come to understand our name?

A New Name from God

My earthly name is Dan, but I will one day have another name. The name I will most cherish and that will most accurately reflect my being is the one I will receive when I stand before the God of the universe. The apostle John said, "Anyone who is willing to hear should listen to the Spirit and understand what the Spirit is saying to the churches. Everyone who is victorious will eat of the manna that has been hidden away in heaven. And I will give to each one a white stone, and on the stone will be engraved a new name that no one knows except the one who receives it."[3]

John was writing to the church at Pergamum. To enter the famous theater of Pergamum, one had to have a ticket, which was a white stone. Perhaps John used this image to remind the church that entry into God's presence requires a ticket that will be further personalized by bearing our new name. In any case, not all is clear. We will be known by a name that is not yet known to us. We will also be fed and nourished beyond our wildest expectations. "Listen to the Spirit," John said, "and be nourished and enlivened by the manna and the intimacy that await us." It is as if God has a spectacular nickname waiting for us.

NICKNAME INTIMACY

I have a name for my wife that not even my children know. It's not a saucy name, but it's private and dear, not meant for use around others. When I utter this name, I am speaking syllables that bring us to a level of oneness that not even sexual union can imitate. Sexual intercourse raises the ante of senses to the point of ecstasy, but the secret name that I speak brings us both a cascade of memories that are wildly nonsexual, sexual, intimate, rich, sad, awful, and glorious. In one name our whole life and history, memory and dreams, past and future open a space in us that no one else can enter. The name is sanctuary for our union.

Even if your own nickname doesn't represent that kind of intimacy, it does create a special bond. In one word, a nickname speaks of a history, a trial, a moment of shame redeemed, or a defeat mocked. In seminary one of my dear friends named me Nahash. It is Hebrew for *snake*. He knew something of my past as a sales rep for illicit pharmaceuticals; he knew I was worldly, insightful, and troubled. As we studied Hebrew together one lunchtime, he heard how my wife, who worked at a restaurant, would take her lunch and wrap it up in her pack to spirit it out of the restaurant so I could have a fine meal the next day. I never knew why the word jumped out at him, but in his glorious southern drawl, he said, "You're a snake, Nahash." It stuck for the duration of seminary. But no one calls me that name, nor would it mean anything to me to have anyone but John Hall speak it.

Nicknames mirror a moment of meaning. They span the past and the future and create a special place of joy in the present. That is why nicknames are not to be used by everyone. They are meant to be spoken by a unique one. So it is with God's naming of us.

He holds a name for us, written on a white stone, to be slipped to us as we kiss his lips. His name for each of us is to be known by no other. I suspect we may be thousands of miles from God's throne when we'll hear our name spoken, a name spoken only by the voice of God. It will call us to his face. Such is the power of a name; it defines us, moves us, and then calls us to the One who is the only name that matters. To know our name is to be at rest in the tender care of God.

As we reflect the character of God into the lives of our children, we are to embrace our name. And as we do, we are called to name those God entrusts to our care.

The Impact of Naming

One of the greatest gifts God gives us is a role in creation. After Adam was created, the Lord gave that first human a heavy and hoary responsibility—to name all the animals.

> So the LORD God formed from the soil every kind of animal and bird. He brought them to Adam to see what he would call them, and Adam chose a name for each one. He gave names to all the livestock, birds, and wild animals. But still there was no companion suitable for him. So the LORD God caused Adam to fall into a deep sleep. He took one of Adam's ribs and closed up the place from which he had taken it. Then the LORD God made a woman from the rib and brought her to Adam.
>
> "At last!" Adam exclaimed. "She is part of my own flesh and bone! She will be called 'woman,' because she was taken out of a man."[4]

God created all living things, and then he told Adam to give them meaning by giving them a name. It is impossible in our world of nearly infinite nomination to grasp the splendor and marvel of that moment. He was to read each animal and then discover in himself the name that best communicated what God had created. God's range of creation is utterly bizarre. One merely needs to visit a zoo to wonder what God was thinking. The baboon is bizarre. The elephant is no less. The aardvark is enough to make one's head spin with the question, "Is God mad?"

Adam was faced with this mélange of beasts and called to name them for a very sneaky reason. He was called to create and, in so doing, to notice that all beings except him had a partner. Every creature had a counterpart and with that counterpart did things in front of Adam that the man, in his single existence, had never conceived. Don't be so prudish. Go to the zoo. Watch the monkeys mount each other and the wildebeests delicately recreate in the fashion that God has prescribed as holy and good. Adam saw the twos, and then he saw them become one—and he was alone, lonely, and desirous to experience someone like him yet utterly, totally different from him. But he had no counterpart, and after a hard day's night, he slept.

When he awakened and saw Eve standing there, he shouted at the top of his lungs and undoubtedly from the awakening of his loins, "Woman!" He named her and thus he named himself. His name (in Hebrew) is *Ish;* she is *Ishah.* She is so like him as to be all but one letter different. But in one letter she is as different from him as he is from a wildebeest. His name for the woman signifies that she is radically the same yet utterly distinct from him. And so it is with all naming. We can only name what we know, but in each naming we stake off new territory that we don't know because it's so different from our self.

We build on identity, similarity, and analogy, and then we move into the realm of the mysterious. There is enormous risk taking in naming what is not yet truly known. We may be wrong. What we do not yet see may ruin us.

Adam calls Eve "Ishah" by name, therefore he evokes meaning without knowing what will come of this relationship. He is drawn to her not only by sight, but now also by sound. He feels the similarity and the inalienable difference about her body and being. The sound of her name arouses desire, curiosity, and pursuit. It draws him into her orbit, and soon he is swirling in the act of re-creation. All re-creation demands this interplay of naming what is known so we can enter what is unknown. What then becomes known throws us further into what is not yet known. Naming elicits more names. And the more we know, the more we are aware of how little we know or understand the person who has been named.

Anyone who has learned a new field or endeavor, from golf to quantum physics, knows this spiral of knowing/unknowing that comes with all naming.

Perhaps those who write fiction or poetry know this most of all. In a book called *Bold Purpose,* which I coauthored with Tremper Longman III, I had the privilege of writing the book's fiction component. It's a study of the book of Ecclesiastes as experienced by six people in a Bible study group. One of the characters, Noah, is a financial analyst and a mess of a human being. The first section of the story describes his passionate commitment to going to bed as early as he could and staying in bed as late as he could. I wrote that section as I sat in bed, covered by a glorious down comforter, secure in the knowledge that the day was behind me and I could escape reality the moment I tucked myself in. At that moment, I was Noah. Today, I am still Noah.

As Noah's character developed, however, there were countless moments when he was not me. I don't think like Noah or make choices as he does. As I wrote chapter by chapter, I found myself thinking through how Noah would encounter the same situation. It was a frightening experience whenever Noah mocked me as I wrote a section of dialogue. He'd say, "That's not my voice. That's your thought, not mine. I'd never say that." Noah almost became a voice in my head. As I listened, though, he began to help me develop a literary character who was quite different from the one I had started with.

There is no Noah in real life. He is and was a creative naming of many people, moments, and internal experiences in my life. Noah is me, yet he and I are not the same. However, it was only in naming his way of being and living that I began to gain some clarity on how I think and live, to read the themes of my own life story. Every person's story has one or more core themes. And every person's story has a different theme even when it shares with other stories some of the same characters, setting, and dialogue.

In order to know who I might be, I must know who I am. To know who I am, I must name the stories and themes of my life and then move forward with what I do know into the realm of what I don't. This also holds true as I raise my children and am raised by them. In naming my children, I may hear the whisper of the name God holds dear for me. To listen for that name I must study my children, name their themes, and delight in the dialogue of naming and being named. The danger in naming is that what we name will eventually come to name us. This happens with our children as they raise us.

Listening to a Child's Bent

If we ever hope to learn the story of each child's life, we must listen to each individual more carefully than ever. We've talked already about hearing our child's true voice. To do that well, though, we must pay special attention to hearing not only what is said, but also what is *lived*. If we pay close attention, we'll see that each of our children is woven from a different cloth; each bears a different bent. It's our responsibility to listen to how each is wired. Paying attention will give us an initial picture of that child's true name, which includes life themes, burdens, and calling.

My older daughter, Annie, was born in chaos and crisis with eyes wide open. She lives her birth well. Let me recount her entry into the world.

My wife and I arrived at the hospital at a respectable 9:00 A.M. The labor room was comfortable, and the television had good reception. I could feel the tension in my body, but we were soon calm. I put the picture of our first "daughter," a wild-eyed springer spaniel named H. Diggity Dog, on the far wall as a focal point for my wife's eventual birthing exercises. We were Lamaze ready.

Our ob-gyn had made a quick visit and then gone to his office. We waited, and the process didn't move along. My wife was four centimeters dilated, but she seemed to be in no hurry to efface. Around 1:30 P.M. our doctor ordered from his office an x-ray to see if there was something blocking the process. The x-ray showed no problems.

By four o'clock my wife was beginning to have significant labor pains, but still there was no effacement. We noticed as well that the machine monitoring the baby's heart rate had begun to plummet from 160 to zero and back. I had alerted several nurses, but they all said that was to be expected. Unbeknownst to us, the doctor had left his office, and about a mile from the hospital his car broke down. For some reason he got out of the car and ran to the hospital. When he arrived he went straight to the heart monitor and within a few seconds began to scream for the nurses and another doctor to help him do an emergency C-section.

Apparently the umbilical cord was wrapped around our child's neck, and every time Becky had a contraction and pushed, the cord was strangling our baby. The next thirty minutes were a nightmare. I recall little, and yet my body still recoils with the memory of each passing second.

Eventually a nurse told me I could see my new daughter. We had a baby girl. I peered through the window, and they brought this tiny peanut of a being wrapped in a blanket to the window. Her eyes were wide open, her mouth intense, and there was not a single tear on her face.

I don't know how long I stared, but after a while the nurse holding my daughter opened the door and brought Annie to me. She asked if I wanted to carry my daughter to the nursery. She carefully tucked her into my arms, and I cautiously followed the nurse's steps. I couldn't take my eyes off my daughter.

Her piercing and haunting eyes stared at me and through me. It was as if she were asking, "What in the world just happened back there? Who are you and why didn't you do something?" It wasn't the last time I would be interrogated by Annie's eyes. Let me fast forward fourteen years.

I was reading a book when Annie sat down next to me and said, "Do I have to spend Thanksgiving with my family this year?" I put the book down and said, "Of course. What are you asking?" Annie has the ability to easily disrupt my peace. She said, "I hate Thanksgiving with my family. I don't want to go through another Thanksgiving Day like that again."

I didn't know whether to laugh, cry, or scream. I didn't know whether to ask what she planned to do or why she hated the holiday with her family. I didn't really need ask because she continued, "Thanksgiving in our house is a time to eat, complain about how much you ate, make strange noises, watch football, sleep, eat more, and then go to bed early. It's a selfish holiday."

I said, "Well, what do you plan to do instead?"

She replied, "I've already checked into whether a soup kitchen would let me come, and they said yes if I can get down to the inner city." I stared into her brown, seeing eyes and knew I was naked and ashamed.

We are called to study our children from birth. Often in the earliest years we begin to see patterns that indicate proclivities, weaknesses, and hard wiring. Some early habits and inclinations disappear. There are some aspects of their being, however, that are as enduring as their names.

We need to watch how our children deal with frustration, pain, pleasure, and success. We see them with peers and with older and younger children. After a time, organizing themes emerge that enable us to tell a stranger about our kids in a few sentences or with a few summarized stories. As we study our children, we begin to see their core themes, burdens, and dreams.

Naming What Is Heard and Known

If we are ever to learn the themes, burdens, and dreams that tell our child's story, we have to listen for what each child tells us about his or her true name. As we listen, we are to name what we see. Naming involves stating not only what we see, but also how it is good, how it could be used for ill, and what we hope for their life. Naming will always enable the child to see in new ways, and it's always most powerful when we can link together a child's themes, burdens, and dreams.

THEMES

If we listen for what is not said, then we can name the silences. It's a tentative and slow process. My younger daughter, Amanda, was utterly different at birth from her sister, Annie. She was a C-section baby who likely came a week or two earlier than she might have otherwise. She was nearly impossible to awaken. If I wanted to see her eyes, I had to thump her cheeks until she raised one heavy lid and then fell back into a somnolent state. As a little girl, she was laid-back and easygoing, rather than intense and wide-eyed like Annie.

Annie was intense but cautious; Amanda was laid-back and fearless. Daily Becky would tell me Amanda horror stories. She climbed out of her fourth car seat, like Houdini, and started to open a car door when she was less than two years old. When she was two she was caught swinging on a chandelier, trying to jump through the railing on the second floor of a mall onto an ice rink.

Most of the events were reported to me rather than being witnessed by me firsthand, but early one Sunday morning, I was reading the paper and drinking a cup of coffee. The house was quiet. I thought I heard the front door open, but I ignored it. I looked out the front window a few minutes later and saw my sweet Amanda naked as a blue jay, standing in the middle of the street right below a small hill. Any car coming over the hill would never have had time to stop. I nearly ran through the front door, screaming all the way to the street. I swept her up, cradled her, and nearly choked her to death with relief and fury.

We have spent countless years naming Amanda's ability to slide into dangerous places with little awareness or concern. She is a remarkable reader who will often read as she walks and who has often walked square into a wall, falling to the floor, without breaking her concentration on the book. We have been terrified to let her drive a car, ski alone, or walk and chew gum. She is enormously kind and wildly sneaky. And she needs to hear that name.

BURDENS

Amanda's ability to walk into danger and do so with grace has enabled her to befriend a number of her peers who are going through their parents' divorce. Having seen the heartache, she is a ferocious defender of children who have lost their voice in the midst of the cacophony of family violence.

The violence is not limited, sadly, to the homes of her friends. Many times she has seen the volatility and intensity of my anger. Once it erupted in the Frankfurt airport when Amanda was thirteen. We had been standing in line for what seemed like eternity when we were forced to move to another line. I insisted that they give priority to those of us who had been waiting the longest. The ticket agent was uninterested in my opinion, and I told her and most of those around that it was rude and unfair. She barked at me; I growled in return. My family was mortified, and the crowd became awkward and silent.

Amanda broke the silence. She said to those around us: "His anger is very unattractive, but most of the time he is a far better man than he is right now." She spoke truth, and the whole crowd relaxed in her courage. I was both mortified and proud. And as life turns in its odd and perplexing revolutions, the ticket agent walked down the line and took our tickets, and we proceeded onto the plane. My daughter is sweet and sneaky bold; kind and willing to take significant risks.

Burdens develop out of the peculiar wounds of life. Burdens intersect with unique skill sets, talents, successes, and failures to turn a child's heart to moments of meaning where she knows or at least senses that she is meant to major in engineering, teaching, or medicine. And, perhaps even more, burdens are associated with peculiar moments and faces, scenes and events that mark a child in a manner we can never predict.

If we name for our children the silences that we see and hear, and then give them the space and time to sync with the passions that are meant to surface, they'll begin to develop short-term and long-term dreams that provide the bass beat for the soundtrack of their life's story. And in allowing our children to grow their dreams, we will be marked and named as parents.

DREAMS

"What do you want to be when you grow up?" is a question we often ask young children. It's one of the ways we prepare them to desire and dream, and to anticipate they will not always be children. We invite children to dream of Christmas gifts, holiday rituals, and special outings. We sometimes give them the opportunity to plan a meal that is entirely of their choosing. Other times we let them browse through a store to pick out their own clothes within a certain price and style range. When we do this, we're teaching our children to desire and dream. It's an enormously important part of parenting.

We must remember dreams are not all full of fluffy clouds and happy faces. Dreams invite desire that might later collapse under the weight of disappointment. Dreams can quickly turn into nightmares. We know that to be true in our own lives; we don't want it to be true for our children. Consequently, we often shield our kids from unrealistic or dangerous dreams. In so doing we are wickedly wrong and extremely right. Our children must learn to dream and be filled with joy—and learn to dream and be afflicted with sorrow. If all their dreams are realized, they'll be bored and arrogant, taking credit for writing their own life's story. If all their dreams die, they'll hate hope and revert to the life of a robot, losing trust in something bigger and wiser than themselves. It's perilous to dream and to allow others to dream.

We are to dream dreams for our children, with our children, and at times, against our children. Amanda is an excellent athlete. Her favorite sport is tennis, and she played first singles position as a high-school sophomore. Her style was maddening. She normally lost the first set because she seemed distracted and tired. It was typically a respectable 6-to-4 loss, usually due to a lack of concentration and fire.

After the first set, she'd become angry if the opponent was irritating or haughty. If the opponent was polite and encouraging, though, the next set was a tossup. If Amanda was angry, she almost always won. If the opponent was kind, she often won, but she could also easily lose the match.

She would then play the final set to the last game and would usually win 7-5 or 6-4. It drove me mad. It was exciting to watch if you weren't her parent and exhausting if you were. I'd shout from the sidelines, she'd scowl—and almost throw the game if I yelled too much. When I kept quiet she played well. From the standpoint of winning, it was best that I either not show up or keep my mouth shut, with no pacing.

But there was a larger issue at play. I wanted Amanda to compete full on, holding nothing back, starting with the first serve. She was afraid to throw caution to the wind and lean into her passion. She is kind and sneaky. Was she playing her own kind of game, or was she refusing to be courageous? Was she living out her name or refusing to own her name?

I wish it were clear. Was I struggling with her play because she caused me anxiety, or did I see, hear, smell, taste, and touch a portion of her life where she was unwilling to dream? Parents are called to wander into the terrain that angels fear to tread—sensing what is and isn't true. We're meant to inflame dreams and then help our children see how frightening and risky it is to lean into their dreams. Yet we must also name how tragic it is to suffocate a dream for the ignoble pleasure of safety and cheap satisfaction. And we won't be able to do this unless we learn to dialogue with our children.

Delighting in the Dialogue

Again, being successful in letting our children raise us relies on carefully listening to their voices, both what is directly spoken and what is communicated through their God-given bent. At no time is this process limited to our voice instructing and correcting our children. Dialogue, after all, requires two voices—with both parties speaking and listening. In dialogue new things rise to the surface that would never have come if only one person were speaking and the other merely listening. It is the joint act of creation—of naming and then being named, hearing and seeing in new ways. In every case, it is rare and holy.

NAMING OUR CHILD'S LIFE

I sat with Amanda on a stone wall after she had won a tennis match. I recounted to her shots and moments in the match that were gorgeous. I described her face and her movement, her apparent strategy and grace. We all delight in being described just as we are in the flow of glory. She described her thoughts and feelings related to some of those moments. It was sweet and restful.

I began to describe when I noticed she was starting to slow down her game. It was, of course, when she was winning. I named how kind she was not to discourage her opponent. I named as well how I wanted to run screaming onto the court to get her to intensify her pace. She smiled and told me how glad she was whenever I somehow found the strength to restrain myself. I described what I was going through as I watched her play ebb and flow in tides of high and low motivation.

The discussion moved on to some of my struggles at work and in my writing. I told of my difficulty in finishing off a project due to my tendency to wander from one responsibility to another. We talked about how hard it is to win and to lose. We talked about the fears of not finishing well and how that fear can keep us from finishing at all.

We had talked for twenty minutes, and it was clear that Amanda was ready to rejoin her friends. I have no idea what good came of the conversation. In her next match, played a week later, her style and outcome didn't change. All I know is that night we dialogued. Afterward I went to the gym and worked out for the first time in a month, and I finished one of the earlier chapters of this book.

BEING NAMED BY OUR CHILD'S STORY

Our family sat down with dear friends and their son in an exquisite restaurant in Australia. We were on holiday and soon to be teaching a seminar at a Bible college. It had been a great day, and it happened to be my wife's birthday. We were celebrating, but the evening's outcome didn't leave much to celebrate.

I don't remember how the conversation turned dark. Our food hadn't arrived, and something had come up about a controversial social issue. I stated a firm position, one on which my daughter Annie and I strongly differed. We began to debate, and the tension whipped around the table like a gale force wind.

My voice was constrained due to the setting and the celebration. Annie, however, was concerned about neither the setting nor my wife's birthday. She was intense and focused and unrelenting. I asked her to calm down, promising that we'd finish the discussion after dinner. I don't to this day know what happened, but she began to cry. Her voice dropped but her tears were loud.

She said, "This is what you do all the time. You state your position loud and clear, and then when I differ you hush me." I knew she was partially right. I said as much, and another shift came. She sobbed, "I am so tired of being your daughter. We get to come to a wonderful place and see really great things, but only because you are teaching at some Bible college. I'm so tired of people thinking I am committed to the same view of God as you are. I'm so tired of people telling me how wonderful it must be to have you as my father. I have no idea who I am because you are so big in everyone's eyes, including mine."

The table was silent. I felt as if I were on stage, not before a small group of Australians and my family and friends, but before the throne of God. Annie was wrong. And she was utterly correct. She spoke out of her hurt and exhaustion, and she spoke of the harm I had brought her. I couldn't defend myself or challenge her assertions. And I couldn't remain silent. I said, "I am so, so sad for what my life and my labor have brought you. And I am so proud that you don't allow my failures to block my relationship with you. Thank you, my love. We will talk more when we are both ready."

And we did. And we will continue to talk as long as both of us have breath. Dialogue enables us to hear not only one another, but also the voice that speaks from behind the cloud and at times as near as our heartbeat. If we delight in the dialogue offered to us by our children, we will begin to let them name us, and perhaps we will start to hear the name God is saving for us.

In both of the dialogues with my daughters, I heard that I am loved. I am privileged to be in their hearts. I can't control them, but I'm honored to have a place to be heard and to hear, to speak and to be spoken to. My children have named me a sinner. Indeed, I am, have been, and will be. Yet their exposure of my sin has helped me name that I am God's rescued heir. I am lost and also found. And somehow my children have honored me with sufficient respect that I can hear from their lips that I am more than desperate and needy; I am also maturing and am now more found in God than I was earlier in their life. They have helped me grow up in God.

My children have named me needy and wise, sinful and bold, silly and noble, angry and tender. They have named me a man who longs for God.

As we consider the power of dialogue, we must of course pursue the ultimate dialogue. Through prayer, we'll come to know the most important name of all—the name of God.

CHAPTER 10

The Divine Dialogue

How Our Children Reveal God's Name

Years ago some dear friends invited me to a day of fly-fishing, and it changed my life. I experienced the grace and power of elegant beauty. The force that is needed to move the fishing line requires rhythm but not brute power, and the interplay with a trout is ballet and not country line dancing. After a few times on one of the most beautiful rivers in the world, I was slavishly hooked.

Soon after this I was invited to speak at a Bible conference in Montana, and I knew I didn't need to ask if it was God's will. Any invitation to fly-fishing Mecca had to be divinely appointed. One of the first nights, I took out my float tube and fishing gear to plunge into the twenty-acre lake behind our cabin. The sun was an orange glow slipping between mountain peaks to the west. I paddled about forty yards off the dock and stared at the western horizon. The view took my breath away.

I put a fly on my line and began tossing it out. I shortened my line and after about ten minutes noticed that a flock of fast-flying birds was dotting the sky. I was surprised that the birds moved with such ferocity. Within seconds they no longer hovered off in the distance; they were flying attack missions over me. It was at this point I realized these weren't birds. They were bats!

I'm allergic to bats. Profoundly. They scare me to death. I began to wave the fly rod above me to mark out the parameters of the no-fly zone. Perhaps you've heard that it's impossible to hit a bat due to their sonarlike capacity to dodge any object in a nanosecond. It's not true. I hit a bat, and it plummeted into the water about six feet from me. It surfaced and began a desperate attempt to find solid footing. I was its only hope. As it moved toward me, I poked it with my rod and tried to move the float tube far from my predator.

The bat was gaining on me when I decided it was the bat or me. I chose me. I began to whack the bat and soon became a bat killer. Within seconds, my line began to scream as a fish took my fly. I was flustered and wanted only one thing: to be out of the water. Now. So I reeled the fish in with no concern about keeping it on the line. As the creature was dragged to the float tube, I picked up the line and saw a fish like none I'd ever seen. Far from a beautiful, highly colored trout, it was thick in the middle with no distinct coloring, and when I pulled it out of the water, without touching it, its mouth opened into a gaping cavern. I have since learned it was a largemouth bass. I didn't care what it was; I only wanted it off my line.

I don't like touching fish. I can take a ten-to-fifteen-inch trout off with some pleasure because of its beauty and elegance, but a big ugly fish with a gaping, toothy mouth? I wasn't about to touch it, so I started to tug on the line to see if the hook would come out. No luck. It was hooked cleanly through the bass's mouth, and my sharp tugs seem to embed the barbed hook more firmly. I wasn't in my right mind by this point, and without a second's thought I began to twirl the line over my head like a rodeo star's lariat. Three times around did the trick, and the fish ripped off the hook and made a sizable plunk in the water.

I reeled in the line and made my break for shore. As soon as I got to the end of the dock, I grabbed my gear and headed toward the path to our cabin. The sky was nearly pitch-black with just a hint of the half-light of the arctic sun. As I walked I noticed a figure sitting in a chair about thirty yards ahead. I prayed he hadn't seen the bat-and-beastly-fish debacle and decided to walk past without saying a word. As I approached, though, his hand reached up and grabbed my arm. He was an older man, in his seventies, grizzled and sharp-eyed. I could smell inexpensive pipe tobacco on his breath.

He said, "Son, I've been fishing for over fifty years. In all my days, I've never seen anything the likes of that." I couldn't respond before he said, "And I just want to thank you." I mumbled, "You're welcome" and made a beeline for refuge.

The next several days I avoided the man. My son and I went fishing each day around 10:00 A.M., and we'd fish until we got hungry around one o'clock. We didn't catch a thing. After three days, my son ran off to go horseback riding as I secured the rowboat and got our gear. That's when the older man swooped down on me. He grabbed my arm and said, "I suspect you want your boy to catch a fish?"

"Yes, sir, I'd love for him to do so. And after three days we haven't caught a thing."

"I know," he said. "I've watched you fish around noon every day, and I suspected you'd do so all week if I didn't say something. Obviously you don't know much about fishing."

"I guess the other evening might prove that," I said.

He laughed gently and said, "The fish don't bite at noon. You've got to be out on the water early, around six in the morning, or late like you were the other night. Take your boy out to that spot by the shore near the reeds and then off the dock about thirty yards where there are some fallen logs and good cover. Use these two lures, be out there before six, and your boy is going to catch some fish."

I could have kissed him. I had the right lures, the best spots, and the correct time, and I felt like the king of the world. When I told Andrew of the gift we'd received, he was nearly ecstatic. I tossed and turned all night, fearful that I'd miss the alarm.

The morning came and we set out. We fished the two spots several times, and after more than two hours I was furious and exhausted. Each time Andrew threw out his line, I knew it was going to be "the moment," and each time he would coax his lure out of the water, I felt my heart sink. This repetition of hope and despair went on until nearly 8:00 A.M. It was time to meet my wife and daughters for breakfast. I felt abject fury. Why couldn't God just cut us the smallest favor and give my son a fish? He divided the Red Sea and raised Jesus from the dead, but my son is stuck with nothing to show for two hours of earnest fishing. As Andrew's impotent fisherman of a father, I decided it was time to end the farce.

I told my son it was time to go. He looked at me as if I'd taken away one of the best gifts of his life. He begged, "Oh, Dad, how about ten minutes more?"

I said, "No. Now. Let's go."

He asked again, "Please, Dad. Can I just throw my line a few more times?" He must have seen my face because he quickly said, "Dad, please, just once more." He knew he was risking my wrath to ask again, yet his desire was so deep he couldn't be silenced.

The story so far makes complete sense to me. The next moment, however, is hard to explain. The Spirit of God spoke to me, not audibly, but also not in a fashion that felt like my mind was talking to itself, and said, "You've killed hope in your own heart. Do you plan to kill it in your son as well?" My reaction was fast and furious: "It's not like hoping in *you* has gotten us anywhere today!" The Spirit's voice was just as quick. He said, "If you are so sure I'm not present, then why do you want to hurt me? You do want me far more than a fish." I could have fallen out of the boat. I looked at my son's face, and I knew I couldn't refuse him, nor could I continue hating hope. I said, "Andrew, you can throw your line five more times." And so he did.

On the fourth throw I felt sick again. Furious sick. The Holy Spirit—or perhaps my own lame brain—had snagged me with hope, and I was a fool to believe. My son started to throw the fifth time, and I turned my back to put the oars in the boat and start rowing us to breakfast. A few seconds after I heard the lure hit the water, I heard Andrew shout, "Dad! Stop! Look!" His rod was bent over near the breaking point. He was tugging on the line, and I told him to ease the tip down and then bring it back up. He did and there was no movement in the water. He had snagged a log. I turned away again and he shouted, "Dad! Look!" I turned a second time and saw his line making sharp angled movements in the water. He had a big one. He fought the fish for about five minutes. My son's little arms were growing weary, and the rod tip was moving dangerously toward the water. I told him to give me his rod so I could help. He looked at me with a gaze of defiance. "What, so you can bring it in like you did the other night?" I decided to let him suffer.

Slowly he tired the behemoth and brought it to the boat. Andrew lifted the line and we were staring at a thirty-one-inch northern pike. I personally didn't like the looks of the bass I'd caught a few nights earlier, but the razorlike teeth of the pike scared me to death. Andrew wrestled the fish off the hook. We measured it and sent it back to the deep, unable to find the camera to get a picture.

We made our way back to the dock, and my son said, "Dad, we have a God, don't we?" He had never said anything like that before. I said, "Son, we do." I felt both the pleasure of the catch, the shame of my disbelief, and the smile of my son's wise words. He then said something that took my breath away. He said, "I know God's name." He wasn't looking at me, nor had he said the words to inform me. He seemed to be saying the words to mark a major moment in his life. I interrupted his thought and asked him to tell me God's name. He said, "My God is called the God of the Fifth Cast."

Prayer is not what we often think. It's not only when we petition God for a fish or the rescue of our child, but it is centrally when we enter a dialogue that leads us to know his name—and our own. Prayer is the birth pangs and the labor of coming alive with God. It's not meant to be antiseptic nor particularly reverential. In fact, the prayers of the saints are lusty, angry, fearful, blaming, honoring, and honest. We can't hear God until we engage him in prayer. There is nothing we do as parents that is more important than praying for and with our children. So, of course, we must answer this crucial question: What is prayer?

The Dialogue of Desire

Prayer is the naming of desire before God. It's a cry for redemption that always begins with avowing the scandal that God is both present and absent. Why do I cry out to him if he is there, fully involved, already active, and omniscient? Prayer is a dirty secret that compels us to ask the hardest questions of faith: "Is he there? Does he listen or even care? Does it make any difference if I pray or not? Why do I care, and why can't I escape him?"

Whether we acknowledge it or not, prayer is a dialogue about the two core questions we all ask every day: "Am I really loved?" and "Can I get my own way?" When I pray, I often attempt to secure both God's love and his permission to do what I want. And as I pray, it is his kind opportunity to invite me to the far deeper desires of my heart. I do long for his love, and I want to do his will. Prayer arouses the deepest questions of the heart and then makes a place for God to speak.

I prayed several times the morning my son and I went fishing. I prayed at the beginning of the day for safety, for a rich and memorable time, and of course I prayed for fish. Andrew and I were safe; our time together was unforgettable; and my son caught a fish. And that day I was the fish caught by God. That morning I prayed a number of other times in accusation and indifference. I prayed and hardened my heart, and I prayed and heard the kindness of the Spirit. Prayer may be eloquent and styled in praise and splendor, or it can be guttural and spitting out blood and broken teeth, but in every case true prayer seeks the face and the name of God.

Prayer draws God to bend down to hear our mumbled desire; prayer lifts us to the throne of God to speak to him face to face. It is the dialogue of desire that draws us to an intimacy and an awe of God that can't be found through any other means. If we choose to persevere in the middle of the mystery of God for our children, then we can do so only to the extent that we pray. Prayer involves at least these four things: lifting the face of those we love (and those we hate) to God, listening to the ache of our spirit, pondering the words we hear, and then welcoming the gifts we receive.

LIFTING THE FACE

For nearly two decades as a young believer, I tried to pray as I had been taught. I had been given as a model the acronym ACTS, which stands for Adoration, Confession, Thanksgiving, and Supplication. It made prayer efficient and well organized. It left me mostly bored and irked at the experience. I still use the structure and recommend it, but back then something was missing.

In the early 1990s, Tremper Longman and I began to write a book that altered my life: *Cry of the Soul.* We wrote it as my life was coming unglued with the death of my father, the death of Tremper's mentor, and the unraveling of my career and friendships. It is the period I first began to pray in a fashion that changed my life. It is also the time I began to fly-fish and discovered that praying is simply another form of play. Due to the tumult I could no longer pray sitting down, hands folded, serenely arching to heaven words that felt preposterous and hollow. Instead I argued, ranted, pled, cajoled, and wept.

It's difficult and silly to rant and weep silently. I'd grown bored with my silent inner monologue. Instead, what I found helpful was to talk out loud and, at times, to yell out loud. I talked to myself, to my father, to my broken friendships, to my wife and children, and every now and then I'd say, "And if you are listening, God, then join me when you want." I know it sounds ridiculous, but a part of prayer, after all, is talking.

I learned a lot, especially when I'd return to my office after prayer and begin to write. Sometimes the writing was a prayer. Other times it was another rant in the form of prose, or poetry, or a short story, or a chapter in a book, or simply words strewn in the stumbling effort to catch up with what I heard God saying to me.

It was during those moments when it dawned on me that prayer is lifting the face of those I love and hate to the face of God. It is the face that marks us as most individual, distinct, and human. It is our identity. To touch the face of an enemy is repugnant. At that time I had a few articulate enemies, and I wanted to scorn their faces; I certainly didn't want to gently touch the cheeks of those who had so deeply hurt me. And to hold their face and lift it to God seemed like an offering destined to crush me. But it did just the opposite. It freed me (at times) to care and to offer my prayers as a gift, an unholy mixture of humility and hatred, desire and demand, and despair and hope to the God of the universe.

Prior to that awakening of prayer, I would say a few sentences about those who I loved or hated, and then I'd finish and know I was no different. I was dutifully faithful, but the exercise led to little but verbiage and dross. But as soon as I pictured a friend's or an enemy's face, I'd feel a visceral change. And when I put my hands on that person's face and focused on his eyes, I'd feel the weight of all that I felt toward the person and what I suspected he felt toward me. And then to speak his name out loud and to ponder his face either silently or out loud would cause me to recall his stories, struggles, strengths, and weaknesses. I'd often feel the weight of his heartache and anger, or I'd hear the passion our great God feels toward him—and it was hard not to join God in blessing those who hated me.

Soon I was praying with greater passion and desire for those who hurt me. It finally dawned on me that I was praying more for those who hurt me than I was for my own family. So I began to name and lift up the faces of my children and my wife to God. Prayer became a sacrifice of praise and desire with the person's face as the offering made before the blazing fires of God's love.

LISTENING TO THE ACHE

To lift a face to God is to hold up to him what is most dear about the person. It is not asking for insight or for change. It is not a humdrum repetition of the same words to the blank silence inside our head. It is a cry and a carrying of our enemy, our friend, our son, our daughter, our spouse to the throne of God. It is in that lifting that I found and heard new levels of my own pride, demands, and fear. I heard the dark words of bargaining and misrepresentation. The more I cried before God, the more I caught wind of the cruelty and self-centeredness of my heart. Oddly, the more I cried before God, the more I felt both the hunger to be what I am not and the sweet ache to know God. And perhaps, even odder, I heard new things about the hurt, hunger, and hope of the person for whom I prayed. That is the power of lifting another's face to God.

God is in the ache. He is in the unrequited desire of the heart. We can't hope to hear God if we refuse to listen to the groaning of the Spirit. If we will gaze at another's face, we will sense the ache. If we are willing to see the arched brows, the furrowed lines in the forehead, the fear in the eyes, the mouth twisted into a sham smile, then we can lift our hurt and confusion to God rather than pretend it doesn't exist.

Seldom have I been exiled to the deep ache of the heart as I was the day I rushed to the police station after my daughter was arrested. At the end of chapter 3, I wrote:

> As I walked the three hundred yards from the ferry terminal to the police station, I asked God for help. And he spoke to me, not in an audible voice and not with a dramatic sign, but he spoke. He said, "Will you offer your daughter mercy or will you offer judgment? What will it be, Dan, my tenderness or your anger?"

As I walked, each step took me closer to the jail and farther from my daughter. Before I entered the building where my wife was waiting, I stopped, closed my eyes, and brought to mind the face of my seventeen-year-old daughter. I held her face in my hands and lifted her to God. I lifted my face as well. No wonder God said to Cain, "Why has your countenance fallen?"[1] He was naming the face for Cain and giving him an opportunity to take that face to its author. Cain refused. Would I?

Becky and I were ushered back to a small room, a cell, with a thick metallic door including a small rectangular opening to peer into the space. I saw my daughter's face turn toward the opening, and her eyes were moist and afraid. The door opened and I walked in. She didn't rise, but she looked into my face. I don't know what she saw, but she leaped into my arms and began to weep. She became a little girl, tears rolling down her face.

The police officer set up the camera to take the mug shot and the ink to record her fingerprints. He read aloud the charges against my daughter, and he remanded her to our care. She had been transporting an open bottle of vodka in the trunk of her car, and it was discovered on school grounds. She was in big trouble. As soon as the first detail of the offense came to us, I could feel my wife stiffen and my daughter tighten. The first blow hit hard. To lift the face of our child, though, we must first be willing to listen to the ache and the accusation. I could see in Amanda's face the anticipation of questions, incrimination, and attack.

My wife's first questions were mixed with the demand for details and the angst of shame. I turned to her, and she was quivering with hurt and fury. I put my hands on her face and said, "It is now that we either believe in the gospel or refuse it. We live either in grace, or we choose judgment." I pulled my wife and my daughter together in an embrace, and for a brief moment the ache was released to God. Prayer is never finished. It is certainly never complete when we merely lift and listen. We are then invited to ponder what we hear.

PONDERING THE WORDS

Prayer is chewing on thoughts before God. Just as a cow keeps chewing its cud, so are we to masticate the words and the Word of God. Meditation means pondering. We are meant to let thoughts roll around inside us. One need only consider the destructive habit of worrying, which is the counterfeit of pondering, to gain a sense of what meditation involves.

When we worry, we rehearse. We go back to the moment of offense or concern, and then we lengthen the time frame of the circumstances. At times we go back in our thinking beyond the start of this particular incident. We then return to the conversation or event and replay the lines, the nuances, and the facial indicators. Then we think about what we wished we had said or hadn't said. We blame. We explain. Then we flip to the future and begin to extricate the implications and consequences. We begin seeing the other faces that will hear about this interaction. Soon the event spreads to a community and to the effect on our reputation. We begin making plans and forming rebuttals and excuses. Before long the worrier is paranoid and exhausted. More often than not worrying leads to more complicated and less reasoned behavior.

Worrying is a form of pondering that has neither lifted the face nor listened to the ache. In contrast, meditation is holding a thought, image, or word in one's hands and turning it over and over to take in the depth, width, height, and breadth of the immensity of God in that single facet that is our focus. If we will slow down and look at one facet, and then another, until we see an event in light of eternity, then every moment will speak a word from God. It is neither magic nor mysticism; it is simply seeing. God has strewn his being throughout the universe and marked every stone and petal and face. God is sensually carved into every situation and especially in the faces of our children.

Every day my children speak to me. Often I listen to them as a sort of parental financier who decides whether they get an extra ten dollars or the car for the evening. But it's different when I listen and ponder their words and faces in prayer. I can do so only if I mark words to take to God in prayer. I can do so only to the degree I study my children as a text to be read with the One who is most apt to help me interpret my children. I can do so only if I write the words down on a scrap of paper and then hold them in the phylactery of thought to gain a sense of what is being said.

There is no creature or creation more worthy of our reflection than our family. Take notes. Keep a journal or a prayer notebook. Cross-reference moments and conversations. If we're willing to drive the little rug eaters a thousand miles a month for every kind of lesson and club and sports program under the sun, why not at least use the time in the car to consider their words as an invaluable gift? It is through the portal of our children's words and their faces that we enter the courts of the King.

WELCOMING THE GIFT

Revisit for a moment that lake in Montana. As Andrew and I rowed back to shore, I knew I had witnessed someone walking on water. A mean-looking monster of a fish had been elected by God to impale itself on a little boy's fishing hook in order to give that boy the name of God. Far more, at least from my standpoint, it was to drag the boy's kicking and screaming father down into the murky depths of his heart to see the glorious and indisputable kindness of God. My son gave me the gift of God.

Join me back in the present, with the three of us standing outside the police station. As I walked to the car that had earlier transported the bottle of vodka, my daughter asked if I would drive. I looked at her and said, "No, it's your car, and I've had a long day." She looked at me and started laughing. She said, "Me too. You drive." She tossed me the keys, and we drove, catching up on each other's day. When we arrived home, I looked at Amanda and said, "This will either be one of the most awful or awesome days of your life. You will likely be grounded for several months, if not more, and how you handle the loss of privilege, the legal consequences, and the shame will likely determine what kind of person you will become. See you inside." Her smile and clear eyes gave me the gift of God.

Our children raise us to the degree that we are willing to receive them as the gift God gave us to mature us to be like him. We can't become that person until we welcome our children home. We can't welcome them home until we have come home as well. As odd as it may seem, it is by inviting our children home that we face how far we are from God. Who is the prodigal in the story of our life? And who is, in fact, the self-righteous elder brother? It is in becoming *both* the prodigal and the elder brother that we are called to the most serious and eternal act of parenting: the freedom to embrace the grace of God.

CHAPTER 11

Welcoming Grace Home

What We Must Embrace to Become Great Parents

T he phone call ended poorly. A friend who had hurt me and called to apologize had just hung up on me. I had arranged for a mutual friend to be in on the call and serve as a buffer. After the call that friend said, "All you needed to do was tell him he was forgiven and then welcome him home. Instead you asked for proof that he wouldn't hurt you again and then slammed the door in his face."

I argued with him. I reviewed all the harm that had been done and the harm this friend could still do. In a kind and compelling way, our mutual friend said, "Your concerns are valid and the assurances you're seeking make sense. But it doesn't change the fact that you slammed the door in his face."

There was a pause. The silence between us lasted. His voice was calm and sincere: "Take a few days or as long as you need. You feel a lot of hurt and betrayal. I'm sorry for not realizing the extent of the pain, but you need to sit with what's in your eye." We got off the phone, and I felt lousy, accused, guilty, alone. Grace waited; I ran.

Grace is a woman with tender touch and strong, sinewy arms. She is a warrior for righteousness. Grace is not lithe and fragile, nor is she abrupt or crude, and at the moment of reception, her presence is fiercely kind. She receives us, but without negotiation and with no inclination to put us on comfortable footing. Instead, she takes utter charge of our being by throwing her arms around us in delight at our homecoming. It is imperative to gain a visual image of the nature of grace. The most fatherly image of God that serves as a picture of grace is found in the story of the two brothers, often called the story of the prodigal son.

When he was still a long way off, his father saw him. His heart pounding, he ran out, embraced him, and kissed him. The son started his speech: "Father, I've sinned against God, I've sinned before you; I don't deserve to be called your son ever again."

But the father wasn't listening. He was calling to the servants, "Quick. Bring a clean set of clothes and dress him. Put the family ring on his finger and sandals on his feet. Then get a grain-fed heifer and roast it. We're going to feast! We're going to have a wonderful time!...

All this time his older son was out in the field. When the day's work was done he came in. As he approached the house, he heard the music and dancing. Calling over one of the houseboys, he asked what was going on. He told him, "Your brother came home. Your father has ordered a feast—barbecued beef!—because he has him home safe and sound."

The older brother stalked off in an angry sulk and refused to join in. His father came out and tried to talk to him, but he wouldn't listen. The son said, "Look how many years I've stayed here serving you, never giving you one moment of grief, but have you ever thrown a party for me and my friends? Then this son of yours who has thrown away your money on whores shows up and you go all out with a feast!"

His father said, "Son, you don't understand. You're with me all the time, and everything that is mine is yours—but this is a wonderful time, and we had to celebrate."[1]

This passage invites us to see that grace performs three functions that we all desperately need. She waits, she runs, and she parties.

Grace Waits

Waiting is one of life's most demanding tasks. It provokes irritation or anger for most of us. There is nothing like standing in line while a lumbering, distracted clerk idly passes one piece of merchandise after another over the scanner. There is nothing to be done but wait, but few of us wait patiently and expectantly. Instead the average human waits with a burning passion to buy the store so he can fire the lip-smacking, slow-witted teenager. Not so with God.

God waits for both of his children described in Jesus' story. God waits for the prodigal, hoping without reason that today his son might return. Was it by chance that the father in the story saw his son far away, or was he out there looking? The possibility that he was looking implies that his heart was set to wait with hope in spite of the high probability that this son was lost forever. It's almost pathological—the father who won't quit, who won't admit reality and get over it.

We see the same willingness to wait for the older brother. The party has begun. Beef brisket is being carved, good wine is flowing, and the music and dancing are in full swing. But no one went out to the field to invite the older son to leave his labor behind so he could join the festivities. The father didn't send one of the servants to fetch the older son. If he had, the cultural norms of the day would have required that the son join the party. One simply didn't refuse the order of the patriarch. But the father waits to allow sin to grow, for the rage to storm, as the older brother returns to the house, without being bidden, to hear the joy of the father's heart at the return of the prodigal.

It is imperative to think about that point. God waits for sin to come home. He allows sin to grow to the point that it can be faced and its cost fathomed. Too many parents are too quick to drive foolishness out of their children. But a wise father waits. He doesn't rush the process of exposing sin, nor does he take extreme measures to rescue the child from his folly. Instead he waits. He doesn't harden his heart or refuse to scan the horizon daily for his lost child—whether the prodigal or the self-righteous elder son—to return. The wise father waits.

Grace Runs

The father sees the younger son coming, still far off, and springs into a footrace for joy. There is nothing decorous or dignified about this. In that day a typical father would not have humiliated himself by welcoming home a disgraced son. He would have waited for the shameful son to fall at his feet and beg forgiveness. If the son succeeded in winning his father's pity, he would, at best, hope to be given the place of a servant. This is what the prodigal had in mind when he pictured himself begging his father, "Take me on as a hired hand."[2] The returning son would become an indentured servant who would remain in that position until he had paid back the debt he owed. Since this son had already received half of his father's fortune, repaying the debt would have meant a lifetime of servitude.

But just the opposite happened. The waiting father lifted his gown and ran to his boy. In that day to raise a gown high enough to run such a race of love, a man would have invoked the ridicule and disapprobation of his community. A man never showed his legs in public unless he was in the midst of war. Then and only then could he "gird up his loins" without fear of shame. But the father didn't care if someone mocked him. His son, whom he feared was dead, was alive! People who know joy can't sit still. They run, jump, twirl. They race and dance.

But notice the contrast in the father's movement toward the older brother, the one who had never left home. With the younger son's bold sin—whoring—one must wait for the sinner to return and then run to meet him. With the older son's subtle sin—self-righteous whoring—one must wait for the sinner and then walk toward him. The father's response to the older son is not the total abandon of joy unbound; it is the steady, relentless pursuit of the real criminal. The story is staggering in its twists and turns, and it is only incidentally about the sinful prodigal who comes to his senses, spills out a pathetic apology, and is wildly accepted by the father. It is really the story of the father's heart for the self-righteous, exhausted, angry, pride-swollen *older* brother. It's a story about our Father's heart for you and me.

Few of us regularly practice such brazen sins as the ridiculous prodigal. Far more often we labor in the overlooked fields of the back forty, exhausted, hurt, disappointed, and quietly rebellious and ungrateful. Rather than being openly shamed by our sin, we resist the sounds of celebration over a remorseful and repentant sinner. From Luke's account, we can't tell where the elder brother landed emotionally; but we know that he was consumed by resentment. And we know that in the elder son's sinful state, the father found him.

The dialogue is excruciating. The father asks, invites, and pleads. He humbles himself and exposes himself to the contempt of his elder son. He is rebuffed and yet he keeps pursuing this self-righteous man. Grace does not push or demand. It lingers. It waits with movement that is respectful yet unrelenting. And still the older brother spits in his father's face!

Not only will grace never turn hard against a person, but neither will she refuse to move toward a sinner to embrace him when the opportunity arises. One son comes and the other son leaves—and the father pursues both with movement that is commensurate with the person's heart. But the father will not force the elder son to apologize by chiding, shaming, or demanding. Instead he will invite his son to the party and then return to celebrate.

Grace Parties

A party is a silly thing. It's a spectacle, an event that seldom turns out as you desire. There is the guest list. You can't invite everyone, so some acquaintances are hurt. You have to seat the guests, but in order of priority or according to disposition? Who should sit with the patriarch? Who should sit at the far end of the table? A matter of a few feet often determines allegiances and political fates. Then you must consider the food and drink. Casual and simple or elaborate and expensive? Chicken fingers or chateaubriand? And then there is the matter of appropriate dress. Never, for one's life, believe a Southerner who says, "Dress will be casual." Dress, above all, is important. The greater the meaning of an event, the more difficult the event becomes. Parties are a lot of work and social politicking in exchange for a few hurried snacks and brief repartee.

If no fights erupt and not too many plates are dropped, then the party was a success. If the host and hostess can sit down and relax for just a moment, then it was a smashing success. Many people are just as happy either not to attend or to show up and then leave without drawing attention to their departure. A party is a big deal, and we all know that big deals have a high cost/small return ratio. There is far more that can go wrong than right.

The party thrown by this overjoyed father would have been the same. Think about the guests. It would be the same people, family, and friends who at some level must have thought the father was first an idiot to give away half of his wealth and then an even bigger fool for running down the road with his gown flapping in the wind. He must be mad to behave this way! However, he is still a rich, very powerful landowner. It's unwise to refuse the food and drink of a wealthy man, especially one so mentally unstable. And why not attend? There might be some excitement. Perhaps the older son will come down from his room, drunk and armed with a sword. Perhaps the best of the father's vineyard will be brought forth on this crazy day. Most of us would attend just to see the spectacle.

But the one thing that makes this a party of staggering proportion is the father's joy. It's not a celebration of glittering earthly accomplishments; it is only the celebration of life. The son was dead and now he is alive. Did he really repent? For the immediate present, who cares? All that matters is the son's return. Tomorrow we'll begin to count the cost.

As hard as it is to embrace grace for one's own sins, it's nearly impossible for those who have been hurt by the repentant sinner who is being celebrated. Early on in my spiritual journey I loved the prodigal, marveled at the father, and felt disdain for the older brother. Now I find I'm irritated at the father, scornful of the prodigal, and highly sympathetic with the older brother who gets the shaft both coming and going. Grace is not sensible, but it makes a darn good story. It touches something in every heart, but it's impractical, even scandalous. The party of God is worse than one of those inexorable, gaudy, wastefully extravagant British royal weddings that we see on television every decade or so. God's party is no more nor less than a celebration of life; it is the pageantry of resurrection. But how in the world do we live that out with our children?

Henri Nouwen in *The Return of the Prodigal Son,* one of the finest books of the twentieth century, bid us to see that we live in the tension of being *both* the prodigal and the older brother. We easily resort to extremes, abusing both the goodness of mercy and tenderness (as in the prodigal) and the requirements of strength and justice (as in the elder brother). Flirting with mercy can lead to overlooking failure, devolving through sensuous excess into license and indulgence, permissiveness and lust. With the other extreme, strength that rightly creates orderliness and structure can be overtightened into a law-bound severity that chokes off gratitude and joy. This one-sided adherence to justice produces the resentfulness of the older brother.

We are called to be fathers and mothers who welcome our children home after their excess. Our calling also includes pursuing our children in the home as they hide in their jealousy and self-righteousness. But we can't welcome or pursue the offender or the offended offender until we know what it's like to be personally pursued by God. We will run to the prodigal and walk to the older brother only if we have experienced that same pursuit by the God who is our perfect Parent—the divine balance of mercy and strength. We are the prodigal *and* the elder brother, and if we embrace the truth of being both, we might hear God invite us to join the party.[3] Then and only then will we become the parents we are meant to be.

The Prodigal Parent

I'm a prodigal. My lusts are as diffuse, contradictory, dark, and unending as my early-morning breath. But the theme of my lust is as universal as all desire: I want Eden. I want a world, a life—wife, children, home, sailboat, job, friends, money—that will take me out of this vale of suffering and suffuse me in the glories of a pleasurable eternity. I want God. It's just that I don't want the God of the Bible who seems to be idling through my captivity with no great rush to end this day of trouble and start a new one.

We must confess the sin of our profound, self-absorbed commitment to be at the center of the universe. It's one thing to nod our head to the fact; it's a whole other reality to confess that we can't attend a piano recital, a soccer match, a parent-teacher conference, or a church service without the loathsome odor of our self-centeredness being the first presence that enters the space. This is not a popular, esteem-affirming notion. It's not only not nice, it's nasty.

I can't watch your child score a goal at the lacrosse game and truly rejoice when my son, the goalie, has been scored on two times by your team. I'm angry at the defenseman who didn't block the shooter and the coach who doesn't seem to yell enough. I'm frankly not that thrilled with a school system that makes lacrosse a club sport and not a school-sponsored team, thereby denying the lacrosse players the advantage of more coaches, equipment, and training. When you get right down to it, I'm ticked at my wife's family for not adding more athletic genes to my children's gene pool.

I'm petty. I'm short-tempered. I'm a victim, a blame-shifter, a ne'er-do-well, and I don't like seeing what's inside me. Instead I'd rather shout at the ref, talk smack with one of the other fathers, grab a hot dog and a soft drink (while secretly wanting something stronger), and then go home and watch television and forget it all long enough to tire of myself and sleep the rest of the dead.

I have to grapple with the fact that I'd love to have a father who'd pay for my season of license and indulgence. In the heart of every sinner is a lurking urge to cut loose and get out of Dodge. On occasion we do that by screaming too loudly at a sports event or talking under our breath about our boring pastor or downing an extra hot dog. There are countless ways we indulge our lusts without being noticed. But there are times when our legions of "innocuous" indulgences eventually lead to more public crimes.

I've sat with countless men and women who hold their face in their hands and confess to an affair, an Internet pornographic fling, an inappropriate emotional entanglement, business crimes, and other sins. They begin to count the cost of the small decisions they made along the way. Often the harmful effect that a prodigal choice has on a spouse, on a job, or on friends increases fast and furious. It's only later that the children appear in the room with startled, disbelieving faces. I sat with one man who for several hours had been coming to grips with his affair when I asked him, "What will you tell your children?" His face turned pale, and he stammered when he said, "I never thought about that. I never thought that I'd have to say anything to my children."

Is it because his children were so unimportant? It's just the opposite. Our children are the mirror image of our best and our worst moments on earth. They are the ones who name us far more than we name them. Such innocent power ought to stop us in our tracks.

To own the fact that we are prodigal parents is to cry out, with the apostle Paul, these three great questions:

Wretched man [wretched person, wretched parent] that I am! Who will deliver me from this body of death?[4]

O death, where is thy sting?[5]

For we are to God the aroma of Christ... And who is equal to such
a task?[6]

I am a mess, and the mess that I am has been redeemed. So how do I live
in the middle of those two worlds—mess and redeemed mess—as a parent?
At all times, parenting involves three core attitudes toward our children.

O WRETCHED PARENT

There is nothing that my son or daughters will do that I've either not done or
would not do if given the opportunity along with the guarantee of not being
caught. Another way of saying this: All sin is common and possible to all
humankind.[7] Therefore we're not permitted the luxury of being shocked or
dismayed by our children's self-centered, indulgent idolatry. It arises from the
seed of their fathers and mothers. Furthermore, we are not permitted to judge
if we have already been judged as equally guilty. And what do we do with our
own failure? It's the core question that will determine how we parent our children. If we indulge guilt and foster a heart of personal condemnation for our
own sin, then we'll allow the murk of our self-hatred to ooze over our children.
On the other hand, if we rest in the embrace of God's forgiveness for our sin,
then we'll more aptly extend the kindness of God's mercy to our children.

DEATH IS DEAD

Nothing my son or daughters will do can alter the plan and passion of God.
There are ultimately no mistakes in life. There are sin and failure, to be sure,
but no mistakes. And nothing that is inscribed in the text of one's life is not
ultimately authored by a merciful God. The illegitimate pregnancy does not
derail his story. The collapse of our dreams or their rise, the kindness and
fidelity of those we love, are all the scribbling of our genius God. Death is
dead. Therefore I can look at temporal life with the inverted vision of eternity. I may not know the ending, but I know the end. And the end is good.
Therefore the ending of my days of parenting will ultimately be the good end

of God's coming. With such good news, not only can I live with the humility of my wretchedness, but I can live in the confident rest of his return.

WHO IS EQUAL TO THE TASK?

We've said before that parents are called to reflect the character of God into the lives of their children. We've also seen that, no matter what we do as parents, failure is guaranteed. So who is equal to the task God has given us? Not I, nor you, regardless of any life transformation or a changed heart. But God is able to use the humility of our confessed prodigal condition to draw our children to the one desire that is the deepest in every heart—the hunger to know God. He is able to use our prodigal anger that demands our own way to reveal to us that we desire even more deeply his will and not our own. The core questions—"Am I loved?" and "Can I get my own way?"—are as inescapable for us as they are for our children. If we simply enter the tension that comes with living in between both questions, then we invite our children to wrestle with the only Father who is perfect and who is able to answer the two core questions perfectly.

When Amanda was quite small, she asked my wife: "Mom, were you always so smart, or did it happen once you had me?" It was so sweet, but so predictably (for a young child) self-oriented. I recall my wife holding Amanda's face and laughing with such pleasure. "Sweetheart, you've taught me just how to parent you. In fact, after telling me how wonderful I am, you usually ask for another bowl of ice cream. Thank you for being so nice, and no, you can't have any more ice cream."

Are you loved? We adore and delight in you (at least most of the time). Can you get your own way? No, not as an invariable rule, demand, or entitlement. Who can answer those questions without flaw, consistently, with no violation of one as the other takes higher prominence? None of us can do so; only God can. However, even our bumbling efforts to do so bring a taste of God to our children. We truly are an aroma of the One who redeems our prodigality.

The Elder-Brother Parent

If I am the prodigal parent, then without question I am also the dutiful elder-brother parent. He works his fool head off, lives by the rules, and asks for little or nothing in return. He harbors resentment toward those who succeed and smug contempt toward those who are not as fortunate. If it's hard to see oneself as a prodigal, it is nearly impossible to face the disease of our self-righteousness.

Perhaps the voice of the older brother reverberates in us most loudly when we hear ourselves say, "It's so unfair! After all I've done for you and you treat me this way?" This is felt not only toward our children but also toward our church, spouse, boss, friends, and even our enemies. "How could you do this to me when I did nothing to you? How could you say such terrible things when you don't even know my side of the story?"

The older brother is consumed with the demand for parity, and equality can always be measured in terms of an account. We can count how many fatted calves the younger brother has been given compared to how much tender beef my friends and I have enjoyed. You've had five and I've had none. My cry rises loud to the heavens: "It isn't fair!"

And God agrees. One of the most disturbing parables of all is the one involving a vineyard owner who hires a group of workers early in the day for a predetermined wage.[8] As the day progresses, more and more passersby are hired to work the vines. Most hearers of the parable would know who came early and who came late. The industrious and wise came early. Meanwhile, those who'd been drinking and carousing all night would sleep late and then struggle to get out of bed to maybe work a few hours before they headed back to the dens of their iniquity. But work needs to be done, and so these slackers are hired.

Then the moment for compensation comes, and, incredibly, all who work in the vineyard are given the *same* wage. The responsible, hard-working boys who had labored all day in the hot sun rage: "It ain't fair!" And God responds, in essence, with this probing and easily answered question: "Do you hate me for my grace?"[9] The honest answer from every self-righteous elder brother is yes! The gospel affirmation is unfair; it's a scandal. God agrees. Indeed, what would be fair for even the most conscientious, hardworking sinner is not to be paid at all. Or, more accurately, what is fair for *everyone* is the unending torment of judgment. But instead we are paid grace according to the measure that God desires to give, not what we are rightfully owed.

Amazing grace, how can it be? Grace wants to dance and drink and eat. She wants to cavort in the wild hymnology of gratitude. And she wants to feed us her pleasure. It is the cry of the father: "Everything I have is yours."[10] We are the angry older brother, complaining about obediently "slaving away" for all these years. And we receive this indictment from our Father: "You have failed to humble yourself by asking to partake of what I have already given you."

The sullen and dutiful elder-brother parent (EBP) serves to be loved without loving to serve. This is every father who works to provide for his family without providing them his love. It is every mother who feeds her children healthy meals without providing a heart to nourish their spirits. It is a terrible conundrum. EBPs slave and suffer, living by the rules and expecting their children to do the same. They hope their children will be good Christians and good examples to others. In the world of the EBP, goodness means "doing right" and then fully expecting a reward for producing all of this rightness. It is the parenting style of the Pharisee who says, "I'm so glad I'm not like that icky, slime-ball, little tax-gatherer. Instead, thank you, God, that I tithe, fast, and vote pro-life."[11]

The EBP fulfills the requirements of her culture far beyond what is expected. She attends PTA meetings, serves on endless committees, and heads up important ministries at church. She wears herself out doing good things and then holds a grudge against the Father for his loving grace. In Luke 15 the older brother pouts and then flogs his father with a well-rehearsed litany of perceived slights. Whenever we turn cold and silent and labor on in the background, we do so with mean strength or vengeance, not the joy of service. The result will be an exhaustion and emptiness that grow inside the bitter and brittle shell of a human being. No wonder most people would much prefer to hang out with the prodigal younger brother. But thankfully, in facing our EBP tendencies, we are reinvited to the party. It is not only the prodigals who get to celebrate. In fact, the wildest dancer on the floor is usually the one who is at the party for the first time even though he thought he had been there for years.

I am an EBP when I count how many days until my children leave home, graduate from college, or get a job so they can support themselves. I am an EBP when I remind them how much their orthodontia cost me and that money doesn't grow on trees. And I am at the height of my EBP standing when I assume that I deserve something better than what I am getting after doing so much for my children.

As hard as it is to come back home after sinning, it's even harder to own up to our children that we must first leave home in order to come home. Not that we need to run headlong into a period of wasteful prodigality. Instead, we must humbly confess that our criticism, judgment, and demands are grievous to God. His grace is scandalous and unfair. And to embrace that grace is to feel a fire burning in our bosom that will turn our duty-bound parenting into play.

Becoming the Great Parent

What separates the boundaries-free prodigal parent and the rigid, self-righteous elder-brother parent from the great parent we all ache to become? It's one thing: the element of play.

The great parent whom every child deserves and whom every one of us seeks to become is a parent who *plays* regularly, constantly, and with passion. She plays with the earnest abandon of a heaven-bound sinner. Great parents play in the pleasure of God's grace and invite their children to the party.

A TALE OF PARENTAL REDEMPTION

My son was nearly three when he began to ski. We had moved to Denver, and my publisher provided us with a winter-long family ski pass. We had little money, so for recreation we skied—a lot. My wife, Becky, was the only family member who already knew how to ski. I was too cheap to take more than a few lessons, so we simply hauled the crew out on the slopes and figured we'd learn by accident. And so we did.

We purchased a harness for Andrew, and I would strap him in like a horse and then use the reins to guide him safely down the slope. Unfortunately I didn't know how to ski. One time he fell on a patch of ice. As I tried to stop, I hit the same patch and slid over his supine body. He howled in tears. When I pulled him off the ground, he kept shouting in his two-and-three-quarter-year-old language, "Fee me! Fee me!" I think he was saying, "Get this harness off me right now and let me ski without the fear of your fat skis crushing me again." I did just as he demanded. Within seconds he moved from an inelegant snowplow to parallel skiing. He was a natural.

It was a beautiful thing to watch this small being floating down the slopes with fearless aplomb. We were so proud. People would shout from a chairlift, "How old is he? He's unbelievable!" And so he was until age six, many seasons later, when he took the worst fall of his life. It was a fall that might have crippled an adult over the height of four feet. His compact and lithe body absorbed the fall, but his psyche did not emerge unscathed. From that moment and for the rest of the season, he lost his balance, confidence, speed, and swagger.

The next season I figured Andrew wouldn't even recall the fall. I was wrong. The first several times out, he was slow and awkward. I had observed many young kids on the slope who transformed their fear into a demanding whine. At least my kids knew not to whine.

We came to a steep intermediate run near the lunch pavilion. Our girls skied ahead to save a table for lunch. Becky, Andrew, and I stood at the top of the slope. He asked me to carry him down. Then he fell down on the ground and began to cry and kick his feet. I was irritated and demanded he get up and ski down. My tone became more terse and angry, and eventually Becky suggested I ski down and wait for them at the bottom. I immediately obeyed.

I waited and watched as my wife coaxed my son to stand up. I knew Becky's voice would be kind and affirming. I watched the two figures for about ten minutes, and there was no movement. I grew weary and decided her gentle approach was not only not going to work, but that it was probably fueling the fires of Andrew's fear. I decided to begin the long climb up the mountain to redeem the situation.

If you ever try to walk in ski boots up a steep slope with little snow and much ice, it will soon be obvious to you that your efforts will be fruitless. I slogged over to the side of the run where there was deeper snow and better traction, but my feet sank further into the powder with every step. It was exhausting. About halfway up I looked at the two figures above me and glared with rage and hope. I wanted them to see my face and decide it was safer to ski straight down the slope than make me walk another step. They wouldn't look at me, so I trudged the final 150 yards to the top.

I dropped my skis and then snapped my boots into the bindings. I began to move toward them, and my wife quickly stepped in front of Andrew. I said as loud as my wheezing lungs would allow, "Move. Your way didn't work. I'll get him down my way." Becky stood her ground.

My wife looked at me with kindness and strength. When I finally reached her, her head slowly turned from side to side and she said, "No."

There was a moment of silence, and she said, "I know you've been shamed by many men who meant the world to you. And I know that is not what you want to do to your son." It was all she had to say. A myriad of faces flashed in my memory, and I felt again the raw experience of being humiliated and shamed by men who really did matter to me. It silenced my anger, and I began to cry. My wife put her hand on my heart and said, "You're a good man." She turned away and in one fluid, graceful movement, she skied down the steep, icy slope.

The flash of her skis and the beauty of her form arrested my sight for a moment, but then I realized that my son was lying on the cold snow and was deathly quiet. I slipped down to him and dragged him over my skis and onto my lap. We were finding our bearings when I said, "Andrew, you saw my face as I was coming up the slope, didn't you?"

He quivered, "Yes."

"And you saw how angry I was, didn't you?"

"Yesss."

"And you were afraid, weren't you?"

"Yes, yesss."

"And you knew I'd make you pay if Mommy had not been so strong and loving and stood in my way and protected you."

At this point his eyes were bristling with tears, and his cheeks were shivering with fear. I looked at him, put my hands on his cheeks, and said, "Andrew, I was wrong. Mommy loved me well and loved you well too. She invited me to see what I had become and what I did not want to be. Andrew, I'm sorry for being so angry. Please forgive me."

The gift my son gave me is incalculable. He put his hand on my heart as he had seen my wife do and he said with tears, "Daddy, Mommy is right. You are a good man."

I can't imagine a greater honor. To win an award for heroism and personal sacrifice must be overwhelming. But what is one to do with an award that comes because sin has been exposed, conviction has come, and the prodigal elder brother has come back to the arms of the father?

Nothing. No thing. One is to do nothing but rest in the arms of one's son. Andrew had forgiven me and blessed me. He had assumed the role of the grace-filled parent. The son becomes father of the man. The man becomes a son of the father as he faces his failure to parent his own son well.

It was now time to ski down the slope. I moved Andrew off my lap, and we stood. He was still terrified. I began to reconnoiter the hill, and I showed him patches of snow that were beginning to form small moguls. I plotted a course and worked through a plan he could follow to get safely down the slope. He made one last plaintive plea: "Dad, please just carry me on your back." I said, "Andrew, do you remember how well I ski?" He smiled. "I know, Dad. It won't work. It's better for me to try alone."

He edged down the slope and eventually began to ski. He hit the first patch of snow and then the second, using the deeper snow to regulate his descent. It appeared he was going to angle his way down the slope with no problem. However, he missed the next several mounds of soft powder and began to pick up speed. He seemed to make a quick decision and glided to the edge of the run where the powder was deeper, but the trees were but feet away. As he popped into the deeper snow, he changed his ski motion and began the pistonlike, up-and-down movement of sailing through deep powder. He looked like a pro. I could not have been a prouder papa.

He reached the bottom and skied to Becky, and they hugged. It was a scene out of *Father Knows Best*. My wife's tenderness and strength had reborn a new strength and tenderness in me. I took in the beauty of the slope, my family, and the God who had saved and protected us. I turned down the slope and made my first turn and then my second. With the third turn my body launched forward, my hands flew out to the side, and for a brief, brilliant moment I was airborne. Like a huge, wingless bird, I flew until gravity reasserted itself, and I crashed head and chest first. I flew up in the air again in a sloppy somersault and then landed on my side with a deft, final face plant. I lay in the snow long enough to be assured that I was still alive and that most of my limbs were still able to move. I finally righted myself, climbed back uphill to retrieve a ski, and slid down another fifty yards to grab the other. I finally arrived at the base to embrace my son and wife in tears and laughter, and we fell to the ground in exaltation.

My son put his arms around my snow-encased body. He said, "Dad, I will never forget what you did for me. This will be a lifetime memory."

And it has been. In fact, several hours after hanging the phone up after I had sinned against my friend who had called to apologize, I was transported back to the top of the mountain. In the hours after the phone call, I had plunged into the despair of recounting how many relationships had been broken and stained by sin—my own and others. It was like walking through a gallery of failures and recrimination. I could see the face of a woman who had made it one of her life callings to destroy me. I saw the caustic face of another friend who said I was not fit for ministry.

The farther I walked down the halls of shame, the more I saw no hope or mercy. And then the Spirit of creativity and play, of remembrance and conviction, brought to mind the moment on the cold and angry slope. That day I had failed my son. This day I had failed my friend, and I remembered failing many friends before him. And yet I can hear God say, "Your son is right. You are a good man. Come home, Son. Welcome grace. Come to the party and play."

There is no calling greater, no task more rewarding or more humbling, than being a parent who can hear the call of God through the voice of his or her children. So come home to your Father. Come home to your children and learn to play.

CHAPTER 12

The Freedom to Play

God's Highest Calling for Parents

The serious work of heaven is play.

—C. S. LEWIS

We parents can fail and *will* fail at almost everything we do. Our most serious failure, however, is not that we fall short of fulfilling certain expectations. Our most serious failure is something that seldom crosses our mind: the refusal to play.

Playing with our children gives them the skills, character, and context for living out their God-given calling. This is by far their most important inheritance, which means that it is callous to deprive a child of a parental playmate. In fact, one of the most compelling reasons to have children is so we can have someone to play with. A good friend once said, "I had children so I could buy the toys I always wanted when *I* was a kid, but not appear selfish doing it."

It's sad that we live in an age consumed with insipid television shows, an overload of professional sports, and other meaningless distractions and still feel that it's selfish for us to play. Play is regarded as a *guilty* pastime, a way to squander some time when we are too burned out to work. We live in a self-absorbed, narcissistic age, but it's still an age of work, not play; busyness, not recreation; and productivity, not Sabbath. To live against the grain of our culture, as we must, the serious parent will spend the majority of his or her time in play—whether we're on the job, running errands, doing household repairs, or playing catch in the backyard. The mature person will see *all* of life, work, worship, and parenting as a form of play.

A Brief Theology of Play

A worldview based on a belief in the Resurrection demands a vision of life that begins and ends with a celebration, a feast of pleasure and delight. This is a party, not some somber affair. The celebration finds its place in all of life— in the joys of sexual intercourse, in the molding of a clay vase, and in the difficult arena of guiding a willful teenager. All of life is meant to partake of the agony of death and the joy of resurrection. It is God's map of life, and all of life can and should be entered into as play.

CREATION, THE FALL, AND HIS COMING

The alpha of existence is creation, and the omega will be Christ's return and the re-creation of the heavens and earth, the banishment of evil, and the wedding feast of the Lamb and his bride, the Church. The beginning involves God's playful creativity, and the end is a party hosted by God where we will eat, drink, and celebrate for at least two bazillion millennia. But what about the time in between?

Creation was followed by the Fall, which ushered in a darkly serious period. This is the life we know, the life of sorrow and loss. As such, it seems naive to call the period between the Fall and his coming kingdom a period of play. How is one to think of a dear friend's body withering under cancer, or a bitter divorce, or unspeakable evils like the Holocaust, the rape of the Armenian innocents, the death of twenty million Russians during Stalin's pogroms in the same breath as the word *play?*

Such horror is not play, nor is it playful—except to the dark side. It is war, pure and simple, for all who are not evil. But evil does not own the beginning, nor does it possess the end. God does. And if we believe he is a sovereign and good God, then even the darkest part of this life's war is ultimately a prelude to a day of full-bodied play that will be ours for eternity.

It is an act of faith and a defiance of evil that we view today as a moment of preparation for eternal play. It is not naive, sentimental, or silly to consider all of this life's war as a form of creative, rest-oriented, passion-enhancing play.

If It Isn't Fun, It Isn't of God

I sat with a therapist who specializes in the area of domestic abuse. She works with women whose faces have been marred by violence and despair. She daily hears stories of rape, assault, and shame. She supervises a clinic, teaches, advocates, prays, and suffers for the women who are abused. She works as well with the perpetrators, treating them with wisdom, grace, and hope. As I told her about my own work in the area of sexual abuse, she said, "We are so privileged to be called to this work. Isn't it fun?"

I knew exactly what she meant. There is nothing in life more fun than destroying evil and growing good in its place. Play enters chaos and brings about order. Armed with structure, tools, rules, imagination, process, theory, and tactics, play confronts what is wrong. It transforms death into beauty— the beauty of seeing a wrong made right, reaching the summit, or scoring the winning goal for your team.

If You Don't Fail, It Isn't of God

All play requires us to boldly enter the unforeseen. If there were no prospect of failure or risk of greater chaos, then the task wouldn't compel our involvement. Play requires us to take risks and open ourselves to the potential for suffering.

But of course it's not all risk and failure and suffering. If there were no possibility of communal joy, honor, and glory, then all of this play would never be worth the effort. Everyone wants to win, and often we do win. It's a cause for celebration. But we touch one another most deeply when we honestly share the path to defeats, failure, and humiliation. The stories of not coming out on top are far more compelling and far, far more connecting and endearing. Listen to a group of teachers, or mothers, or even avid golfers, and you will hear an idiosyncratic but understood language and nuance. There is the exchange of information and the sharing of both successes and defeats. It is the interplay of defeat and success, chaos and order that draws our passion.

Likewise, every time we play with our children, we invite them to take risks within the safety provided by wise rules. We are called to lead them to take a reasonable risk to achieve a greater good.

Play as Risk Within Rules

For years I've taken small groups of men on fly-fishing trips to talk about the significant matters of life. On one trip I took along my son, Andrew, when he was twelve. He would serve as our gofer, and then after the other men returned home, Andrew and I would begin our sex education discussions. I was nervous as a cat as I anticipated the sex talks. I've taught in front of ten thousand people about physical intimacy with infinitely less stress than I felt as I packed a few books and tapes to use in our first birds-and-bees conversation.

The trip was a huge success. The men loved Andrew, and he was a supreme help to many who had never fly-fished. He is patient, kind, and knowledgeable. The last day of the trip we fished in the Frying Pan River near Aspen, Colorado. It is a swift and demanding river. I fished hundreds of different runs that day, but Andrew chose one forty-yard stretch of water to work over and over. A fly-fishing guru in our group named this most productive hole, which held a large number of brown trout, Andrew's Throne Hole.

It was the end of the day, and the men were filtering back at the prescribed departure time. That's when Andrew beckoned me over to his position. I came behind him expecting to be told to watch as my son threw his last few casts. Instead he gestured to the hole and said, "You fish it, Dad." I lengthened my line with a few false casts. Then the fly dropped right at the intersection of the fast-moving water and the quiet holding water of the trout. I failed to raise a fish, however, and Andrew patted me on the back. "I thought for sure you'd get a strike on that one," he said reassuringly. The next several tosses were inept. I was tired and wanted to leave, so I gestured for my son to finish off the hole for me.

His casts were relaxed and accurate. I glanced at a handful of men watching from the riverbank. Their eyes were fixed on my son. He worked his fly up the flow until he was just behind a big boulder. On his third toss, a large trout swallowed the May Fly. Andrew let the fish descend, and then he set the hook. It was effortless and impeccable. The fish ran right toward us. Andrew lifted his rod and stepped back as he reeled in the line. I was just to his right, and he ordered me to move. His voice was direct and inoffensive. I took three steps back and, without missing a beat, Andrew said, "No, Dad. I mean out of the water. This fish is going to run." I moved to my right a few more steps and came out on the bank. One of the men put his hand on my shoulder and said, "He's quite a fisherman, quite a boy. And you're a good dad to move so quickly."

Andrew landed the sixteen-inch cutthroat to the applause of a choir of men. It was glorious to see him net the trout and hold it up to their delight. The group of men left for home, but my son and I stayed to do more fishing. A day later we were alone in the mountains, and I introduced sex as our topic for discussion. Andrew looked no more thrilled than if I had told him he was going to spend a day in a dentist's chair.

The first session lasted an hour before we took a break. When we resumed Andrew said, "Do you have to keep talking about the vagina and the penis?" He was referring both to the entirety of the sex talk and to the continued use of those specific words. I told him I was open to using other words, but I needed to know what terms he wanted me to use.

We were playing—deadly serious play. He wanted to avoid the topic all together. I knew his future depended to some degree on how he dealt with his sexuality, which included what he did with this conversation. The rules were simple: We will have this conversation, and it will go on for months, even years. We will talk about the facts of sex, the heart of pleasure, and the character of a man who is called to faithfully give his body to a woman for a larger purpose than his or even her pleasure.

How we enter the topic and how he engages the material—including what language or questions or concerns he addresses—is his part of the play. I threw him the ball, and he caught it. It is this risk—the call to engage, create, and transform—that energizes life.

For several minutes, Andrew remained quiet. I finally asked him if he thought I was going to go away. He smiled and said, "I hoped so. I guess we're going to stay with sex, huh?" I nodded. He looked at me and replied, "Well, how about changing the penis and vagina to trout and net." I was so stunned by the acuity of his metaphor that I just stared at him.

I was no longer the adult and Andrew the child. He took the playing field and decided to engage the process. I taught him a great deal about sex. He taught me even more about risk, compromise, and communion.

All play starts with a structure of normative rules and procedures about how the game is to be played. But once the game begins, opening the door to the chaos of uncertainty and struggle, then a new creation will occur. And it is good until it must be torn down again and then rebuilt for an even greater good to grow. Play begets greater good. And the fruit of playfulness is always meant to invite others to the generous bounty of the party.

Play as Prodigality

Play is prodigal, meaning that it is overabundant, without limit. The prodigal son of the Bible left home so he could operate without the limits of social constraint. In a far land he spent his father's money on riotous living. The father who received him back, however, was even more prodigal. He met his repentant son with limitless grace, which he lavished on him in the riotous frivolity of love.[1] Play is equally excessive. It invents and multiplies options and possibilities. There may be a fixed number of musical notes and time signatures, but there is a limitless number of combinations that produce an infinite variety of melodies. Annie Dillard writes:

> Nature is, above all, profligate. Don't believe them when they tell you how economical and thrifty nature is, whose leaves return to the soil. Wouldn't it be cheaper to leave them on the tree in the first place? This deciduous business alone is a radical scheme, the brainchild of a deranged manic-depressive with limitless capital. Extravagance! Nature will try anything once. This is what the sign of the insects says. No form is too gruesome, no behavior too grotesque. If you're dealing with organic compounds, then let them combine. If it works, if it quickens, set it clacking in the grass; there's always room for one more; you ain't so handsome yourself. This is a spendthrift economy; though nothing is lost, all is spent.[2]

Part of the huge risk of life is its endless possibilities. If you don't play tennis, you can play lacrosse. If you don't like sports, you can play chess or knit, collect stamps or feed the poor, translate the Bible or garden or swim or pray. Or you can do all that and still love baseball. Life—and all play—is prodigal. To try to break down the options makes the head and heart spin. But you must choose, and in making a choice there is a path not taken and a chosen route that now limits you while also expanding a new range of choice. The acts of choosing and then acting on our choice change us.

We can't play without being transformed, created, lost, and found. Writer and poet Dianne Ackerman writes,

> Whatever artform one chooses, whatever materials and ideas, the creative siege is the same. One always finds rules, always tremendous concentration,

entrancement, and exaltation, always the tension of spontaneity caged by restriction, always risk of failure and humiliation, always the drumbeat of ritual, always the willingness to be shaken to the core, always an urgent need to stain the willows with a glance.[3]

You can't have children without being transformed. You can't let them play with your life without becoming an entirely different person, who then proceeds to become another entirely different person as you allow your children to mess with you. Every day that you get up and help your children dress, eat breakfast, and send them off, you enter a realm of prodigal play that is more serious than life itself.

Play as the Serious Work of Earth

It is tragic that play is viewed as a child's domain and perhaps even more tragic that child's play has been recast into adult terms of competition, achievement, and power. One rarely can attend a kids' sports event without being sickened by the abusive language on the field and off, language usually generated by adult voices. Winning isn't the only thing, but it's the anointed god of a spirit-less enthusiasm that pervades all gaming cathedrals, from Little League to the major leagues. Nothing is more serious to many Americans than their sports team; it is their sacred idol and the focus of their fanaticism.

Studies have shown a higher incidence of spousal abuse in cities hosting a professional football game. Some fans take their disappointment over a home-team loss to violent extremes. Baseball umpires feel the culture's disdain for authority. Coaches, on the other hand, are our benighted fathers. The team itself is our brother and sister. We suffer humiliation and exaltation at the rise and fall of their—and, by extension, our—fortunes. The game just past, and the one to come, become the detritus of our water cooler conversations and the fodder of our immediate hopes and dreams.

Sports are not only serious business, but also serious venues for our escape from the ordinariness of daily life. We live not in the age of anxiety like the '50s and '60s, nor in the age of depression as in the '70s and '80s, nor in the age of narcissism as in the '80s and '90s. We have entered the age of dissociation. We don't want to be present in the midst of the mayhem and mean-spirited divisiveness of our day. We are too despairing and self-absorbed to do much about the terror and uncertainty of our day. It is easier to remove ourselves mentally and emotionally from all that is unsettling and unpleasant. We huddle, hide, and hibernate.

And we do that best when another does the suffering on our behalf. It's as if we have outsourced danger to our professional athletes or our soccer-playing children. They can—on our behalf—put on the uniforms and descend to the field to see who comes out the victor. From the safety of the sidelines or even from our family room, we can yell at them and for them. We have become a world of watchers, voyeuristically snatching the passion from other people's play. And the dissociated observer always becomes the critic, proclaiming the expertise of a seasoned armchair quarterback.

It's as true in sports as it is in the church, government, or the arts. If all we do is observe, if we never join the game to risk and get dirty, then we will distance ourselves from the play and, in time, turn against those who perform. Deadly serious judgment—often harsh, cold, and cruel—comes from those who stand on the sideline and refuse to enter the game. Likewise, the most critical and judgmental parents are those who refuse to play with their children.

Contrast that with parents who enter the fray, who recklessly plunge into the thick of life with their children. Those who play know the honor of engagement no matter what the outcome. Adding one's blood and voice to the process changes the soul of the person and the spirit of the event, even if the effort ends in perceived failure.

This view of play strikes painfully close to home. My wife and I spent years helping create a school that we then had to watch collapse. In that horrible, unending moment, Becky said to me, "Remember to rest. It's just life and we live only once." I looked at her with shock and amazement. How could she say, "It's just life"? Here's how. This is the *only* life we experience on earth, and it's a shame to squander it by not surmounting great obstacles and suffering enormous, exhausting burdens. This full-throttle engagement of life is the great legacy and inheritance we must give our children.

You may recall the story about my daughter Amanda, who was caught at school transporting alcohol in the trunk of her car. After many months of being grounded by her parents, she still had to perform court-ordered community service. One of these activities joined her to a community group that sends volunteer workers to several Siberian orphanages. Amanda heard an account of how each American teen has the care of a single Russian orphan for nearly a week. During that week the teenager joins the orphan in playing games, making crafts, riding on teetertotters, and swinging on ropes. Far more important and life-changing than all of the games and activities, though, is the concentrated week of offering an orphaned child a teenager's face and attention that is all theirs, and not shared with any other child.

Amanda seized this possibility with vigor. She had given up some troublesome relationships. She had stopped attending certain social events. A life that no longer moves in one direction can slow down enough to change. For some, such change involves hitting a wall. But once the life has stopped going in a certain direction, there must be a turn and a picking up of speed toward another destination. During Amanda's months of slowing down—and once hitting a wall—she began to listen carefully to the things that brought her joy and sorrow. She began to listen to the whispers of a new name being given to her; she moved in a new direction and began to play with new possibilities.

The trip to the Siberian orphanage would require raising $2,500. She would have to learn about the Russian people and the unique struggle of the orphans. She would have to give time to car washes, meetings, and reading. The day came and she flew away, our dear, precious little jailbird. We ached and worried. She lived and served. She came home a different young woman.

In her return letter sent to those who supported her trip, she said, "I never knew the heart could ache so deeply or love so richly."

Play is not an escape from the heartache of reality. Instead it involves embracing the outcome of all reality. It mimics the open-armed father who welcomed home his wastrel son, no questions asked. It echoes as well the commendation of a wealthy master to the shrewd members of his staff, recounted in a parable of Jesus: "Well done, good and faithful servant!... Come and share your master's happiness!"[4] All conversation and activity is meant to take its rightful place in the bigger party of life. There is no better gift we give our children than an invitation and opportunity to play.

Playing with Your Children

Playing with your children includes but exceeds throwing a ball, playing with dolls, or digging in a sandbox. It includes reading stories, watching television, training a puppy, running errands, and weeding the garden. Play occurs whenever you risk the entry into the unknown, adhere to certain rules, expend energy, and gain a sense of satisfaction, even in defeat, to grow what is good and to destroy what is evil.

But let one thing become clear: Play requires more time and demands more engagement than does our work. The process of playing well together is more important than the task or the outcome. For that reason, work is onerous yet efficient, whereas play is fun and prodigally wasteful. You can weed a flowerbed far faster alone than you can by involving a child in the process. One can ride a bicycle far faster and farther without the encumbrance of children. A walk will produce more physical exercise when undertaken alone than it can if a child is tagging along asking questions about trees and birds and whether you saw that lizard dart into the rocks.

Play is ridiculously inefficient. It splurges and spends, often without any apparent return on investment. That's why we must remind ourselves of the blessing of the process and not look for any measurable outcome of the effort.

I have a boulder that I sit on at a favorite river I see only once a year. I may sit on that rock two or three times during the week that I am fishing this spot, but its presence is inscribed in my palm, its grandeur always near in my mind. I go there when I need to feel the water rush by and cleanse my soul of the debris of my crowded, self-important life. Play gives us a field, a favorite fly rod, a pair of boots, and space—sacred space—to re-enter when our days become long and cold and exhausting.

If I remember my own holy places of play, then I can look ahead and know that I may be happy again as I was once before. All play requires a vision for tomorrow. That is how it produces and sustains hope. That is how it boldly risks a picture of a desired future in the gritty demands of everyday life. Every trip to the soccer field for practice is the promise of the coming game. Each game is a risk for the coming championship or the athletic scholarship or even just the dedication of the player who practices harder than others but knows the suffering of riding the bench. All that driving to all of those practices, year upon year, can be a meaningless passage of miles to keep arriving at a playing field, or it can be the meaningful play of today that anticipates the opportunity of tomorrow.

Am I now speaking about the player or the parent? It should be both. But sadly, what I've described is most often the child-player, not the parent-cheerleader-confessor-driver-medic. Play requires dual participation. It's not play unless a parent joins with the child in the party. I am meant to rant and rave, to cry and shout and pace nervously—all because of a single missed tennis shot. I am also to pour myself into challenging my son at a computer game and helping my daughter plan a trip to Russia.

In those moments I must remember the love of play; I must risk dreaming for my child; and then I must invest and risk my life in the endeavor. Such play always requires a certain involvement on my part: that I watch and admire, and that I join and lead my children in the serious work of heaven. Or, I should say, the serious play of heaven on earth.

Watching and Admiring

"Look at me, Mommy! Watch this!" Those words echo from a playground (interesting word) like the refrain of a timeless hymn. Play is meant to captivate. As a three-year-old twirls in her new dress or as a hulking seventeen-year-old teenager puts on a uniform for the big game, they are dressed not for success but to be admired.

The "look" we see in the eyes of observers can make us or break us. It is life or death, but one of the key elements of all play is to be watched and to have the outcome known to others. It is the anticipation and the uncertainty that builds drama, and it is the outcome that for a moment stops time in the power of the performance. The five-year-old who is preparing to launch herself off a swing does so with as much ceremony and anticipation as the astronauts who solemnly proceed single file out of the staging area into the spaceship that will catapult them beyond the sky. Why such pomp and circumstance? It is no different than the child who shouts with glee, "Mommy, watch me!" The child is saying, "I am about to do something really dangerous and extraordinary—and if you watch long enough you will be amazed, dumbfounded, and so very proud of me."

It is the same at a piano recital, at the opening of an art exhibit, and at a wedding ceremony. "Watch me, Mommy! I am/We are about to do something really amazing!" There are some who believe this may add to a child's cumbersome self-absorption—it can. But far more it is the true glory of play: We have come to watch you and be amazed by you.

Amazement is the antechamber of admiration. To admire is to humble oneself before the splendor and glory of another. It is the one thing a narcissist can't permit. It is the obverse of envy and jealousy. Admiration blesses the other as being and becoming what we are not. It names uniqueness without attempting to bring it down to our status. It is the finest form of accolade.

Every child longs to be the apple of her parent's eye, not due to a perfect performance or even as a result of hard work, but simply because she is cherished. She may cross the finish line in last place or return home filthy after squandering half the family wealth, but she is still a sight for sore eyes. It's when a parent's eyes light up that play has reached its moment of fulfillment. "Watch me, Mommy" doesn't end when a child is six nor even seventy-six. It is one of the core cravings of the human heart. I am meant to be prized. I am meant for delight. It is play that gives us the context and opportunity to be admired. But play also calls a parent not merely to watch the game from the sidelines, but to join and lead a child to life.

JOINING AND LEADING

A heart that loves play can't remain on the periphery; it must join in the dance and celebration. It's never enough to drive one's child to a music lesson and catch a few moments of rest as he blares his horn in someone else's ear. One must join or it's not play. Sadly, few parents play with their children after the first few years of life. We may drive our children to play, but we seldom join in the serious act of incarnate play.

Does that mean parents should join an adult soccer league if their daughter loves soccer or take up the violin to accompany a future virtuoso? Perhaps, but if we horn in on all they do, we take away their opportunity to grow in independence and autonomy. But there must be a playful joining that enters their world and that invites them to enter our universe.

It can be a sport. It can be homeschooling. It could be a love of stamp collecting, knitting, nineteenth-century romantic literature, or digital photography. It just has to be something that you love, your son and daughter love. In every case, it's a joining that calls the parent to lead.

A parent leads by modeling the reality of independence and intimacy. To do so demands courage and risks loneliness and failure. Leaders must embrace personal failure and then repent. To repent means to humble oneself before the deed done or undone and live in light of what was meant to be. Repentance is living the truth that we can't live the truth and asking for help in the face of our dependency. Repentance sends us back home to the waiting arms of our Father; therefore, true repentance is the precursor to redemption. True leadership not only repents but receives the even more humbling call of the party to celebrate with a God who bears failure as his own rather than extending it to us as our due.[5]

Leadership in any endeavor, therefore, requires the risk of decision making and bold engagement that invites failure. Once this dynamic is embraced, then a true leader accepts the welcome outcome with the unwelcome. She gladly rejoices in the good and refuses to deny the harm. A leader lives not on success but on the inevitability that she must strike out, pick up the bat, and take another swing. She does this with the awareness that, in spite of sin, grace abounds, and we are called to marvel in God's grace.[6] Such marveling leads to bone-deep gratitude.

Gratitude is a precursor to creativity. The more freedom I know in the face of failure, the more I am willing to use the broken shards of my last attempt as the raw material for today's new work of art. This is the dividing line between rigid and legalistic parenting and generous, grace-filled parenting. The more we set as our goal to parent with perfection, the more we will not only fail, but we will fail with rigidity, anger, and guilt. We will come to covertly hate our children since their presence in our lives is the occasion for what we perceive as our greatest failures.

On the other hand, the humble, open-handed prodigal parent knows that he can't do it well. He recognizes that failure teaches us far more than success ever will. My failures invite grace, gratitude, and, even more, creativity. True leadership moves from gratitude to re-creation. I must re-create with my children, especially in the face of my failure.

A Taste of God

It was my son's twelfth birthday party celebration. It was a fun night filled with presents, cake, and stories. Toward the end of the evening, my son and I traded hits to the arm. His growing strength delivered a nasty punch that really hurt. I whacked him back and said, "We're done." He hit me again and there were tears in his eyes. I was furious and told him we were going to end the frivolity. He stared at me and his lip quivered. He blurted out, "You've always got to do something to ruin a good time. You've ruined my birthday." He ran upstairs with cold fury.

My wife and two daughters looked at me in disgust. Annie spoke first. "Dad, he has a point. You often take things to extreme. I think you hit him too hard." Amanda piped in and added, "You don't seem to be able to let a good evening just end without making people upset with you." Becky just stared at the train wreck. I felt caught—guilty, confused, hurt, falsely accused, and aware that something important was being said that was both true and untrue. I could either defend against what was untrue or move into the humbling matters of what was said that *was* true.

I went to Andrew's room and found a locked door. I couldn't demand it be opened, nor could I let his anger win by hiding. Parenting is often a process of failing and then failing again in response to the original failure. As the failures mount they become patterns that are so regular they are mostly ignored. Then they are either excused without forgiveness or harbored without awareness. In either case, they add scar tissue to the original wound.

Standing there in the hall, I silently confessed to God. But I didn't feel the joy and wonder of being forgiven. I've known that joy in the past, so I banked on the interest those other events had brought us all. I knocked on my son's door and said, "I failed you terribly. I still don't understand the depth of your anger, and I won't be able to do so until you talk with me. If you won't talk, then at least open the door and let me stand before my wife and daughters and tell them in your presence that I failed you and dishonored you."

Leadership moves forward and fumbles. It confesses. It receives what it doesn't deserve, and then it risks again another series of downs in the game. Andrew wouldn't come to the door, and I told him he had five minutes to decide. At the end of the five minutes, I would open the door and we would talk even if he chose not to speak. Was I in error again? Should I have just let the interaction cool and assume things would get better tomorrow? When is retreat the better course? I don't know. I only know that I had hit my son too hard, changed the rules in the middle of his experience of violation, and cast a dark shadow over his birthday.

I was wrong, but I was still his father, and he was my son. I was still the one who was meant to lead, even if I was now called to lead forward due to my sin. Sin never releases us from our calling to lead. We are not to lead with denial of our failure, nor is our failure an excuse not to take hold and create. Right or wrong, we still have to lead.

Five minutes passed, and I said, "I'm coming in. Please unlock the door and let me face you man to man." I could hear his chair move back, and he ambled slowly to open the door. He looked down at the floor. He was working hard to hold onto his cooling anger. We sat on his bed and eventually tears rolled down his cheeks. I put my arms around him, and he sobbed. I was still as confused as I had been when he first erupted. I couldn't figure out how I had provoked a flurry of adolescent rage, nor did I understand why he was suddenly a gentle boy crying huge tears.

But I do know this: Andrew needed, desperately needed, a father who could be humbled and yet would not be weak; who could surrender while also fighting for his soul and our relationship. He needed a taste of God. I need that desperately as well—from my son and with him. I knew God was present, in the room and in the sinews of our touch as we held each other.

I am, and will always be, the father of Annie, Amanda, and Andrew. It is my most important distinction and honor, second only to being the husband of Rebecca. But I am a desperate, frightened father. I am also a wayward prodigal and a self-righteous elder brother, both of whom are welcomed to a party that is entered most deeply through the doorway of my family. If I will but heed the invitation, obediently walk through the door, and receive the heartache and glory that awaits, then I will be not only a better father and husband, but a human being whose children have raised him up to a deeper, more honest knowledge of God.

Through success and failure, through joy and sorrow, through laughter and tears—through it all, our great and wild God still uses children to raise parents.

Notes

Introduction

1. See Matthew 18:3.

Chapter 1

1. Jon Walker, "Family Life Council Says It's Time to Bring Family Back to Life," *BP News,* 12 June 2002. Found at www.bpnews.net.

Chapter 2

1. See Ephesians 5:1-2.
2. See Luke 13:34.
3. See Hebrews 12:5-11.
4. See Leviticus 19:2; Matthew 5:48.
5. The Bible states that providing needed discipline is not an option (see Proverbs 23:13-14). It further states that a child without discipline is unloved (see Hebrews 12:5-11 and Revelation 3:19).
6. See Ecclesiastes 4:4.
7. James 1:5, NIV.
8. See Mark 12:28-31.
9. See John 17:6-19.
10. See Luke 15:11-32; 18:18-25.
11. See Hebrews 5:8.

Chapter 3

1. For more on this, see William Strauss and Neil Howe, *Generations* (New York: William Morrow, 1991) and Strauss and Howe, *The Fourth Turning*

(New York: Broadway Books, 1997). These respected researchers do not develop in detail the theological and psychological issues related to the cycle of generations. My adaptation of their findings is not to be blamed on their compilation.

2. Hosea 13:4-11.

Chapter 4

1. I will return to my daughter's story in chapter 10.

2. Of course my critique of the self-help industry reeks of insincerity because this book is written for those who are seeking help. So allow me a disclaimer: This book will not revolutionize your life; it will simply set you on the path to doing what you always wanted to do.

Chapter 5

1. Ecclesiastes 4:4.

2. The scriptural basis for this ethic is found in Leviticus 19:18; Romans 13:9; Galatians 5:14; James 2:8; and elsewhere.

Chapter 6

1. See Proverbs 13:12.

2. See Jesus' warning in Matthew 7:15 regarding false prophets and Paul's warning in Acts 20:28-30 regarding false teachers.

3. See Jesus' warning in Matthew 18:6 about causing children to lose their faith.

4. See Malachi 2:15-16 and Acts 20:28-30.

Chapter 7

1. See Romans 1:20-22.

2. Psalm 62:11-12, NIV.

3. Jeremiah 31:20, NIV.

4. See Genesis 1:28.

5. See Genesis 3:6-10.
6. See Genesis 3:11-14.
7. Galatians 3:13.
8. Matthew 27:46, NIV. See also Psalm 22:1.
9. See 1 Corinthians 1:18-31.

Chapter 8

1. Proverbs 17:25.
2. Proverbs 23:24-25.
3. Proverbs 27:11.
4. See Proverbs 17:25.
5. Romans 5:2-5, NIV.
6. See Romans 8:26-27.
7. See John 14:25-26; 15:26; 16:14-15.

Chapter 9

1. See Revelation 2:17.
2. See Psalm 62:11-12, NIV, in which the psalmist gives us a succinct description of God's character: "You, O God, are strong, and … you, O Lord, are loving."
3. Revelation 2:17.
4. Genesis 2:19-23.

Chapter 10

1. See Genesis 4:6, RSV.

Chapter 11

1. Luke 15:20-23, 25-32, MSG.
2. Luke 15:19, MSG.
3. See Henri Nouwen, *The Return of the Prodigal Son* (New York: Image, 1994).

4. Romans 7:24, RSV.

5. 1 Corinthians 15:55, RSV.

6. 2 Corinthians 2:15-16 NIV.

7. See 1 Corinthians 10:13.

8. See Matthew 20:1-16.

9. See Matthew 20:15.

10. Luke 15:31.

11. See Luke 18:9-14.

Chapter 12

1. See Luke 15:11-32.

2. Annie Dillard, *Pilgrim at Tinker Creek* (New York: Harpers Magazine Press, 1974), 65.

3. Dianne Ackerman, *Deep Play* (New York: Vintage Books, 1999), 136.

4. Matthew 25:23, NIV.

5. See Romans 5:8; 2 Corinthians 5:21.

6. See Romans 5:20-21.

Acknowledgments

The labor of this book came during the birth and the first few years of life of Mars Hill Graduate School (www.mhgs.net). The birth pangs of both enterprises have been far more painful than I could have imagined. Men were never meant to give birth. But many dear friends and colleagues extended levels of care and patience far greater than the pain endured.

To the staff of WaterBrook Press, especially Ron Lee: Thank you for patiently helping me discover what I really wanted to say.

To Kathy Helmers, my literary agent: O friend, thank you for believing through so many miscarriages that there was a book to be born.

To the board and my colleagues at Mars Hill Graduate School: How sweet it is to weep and laugh with you.

To Linda, Samantha, and Allyson: O brave caregivers, gatekeepers, conscience, and friends, thank you for keeping me somewhat sane, on the road, home, and alive.

To Tremper Longman III: Thank you, dear friend, for knowing how to hear my heart's truest word.

To my children, Annie, Amanda, and Andrew: May you breathe the Spirit, wrestle with kingdoms, and eat and drink to His glory.

To my wife, Rebecca: Plantation Hospital. Goshen Hospital. Cold metallic bed. Surgeon's knife. Terror. Birth. Three times you've introduced me to the face of God. Three times and three more you've housed a terrifying gift from God. Each time your beauty has soared, and your presence has showered us with glory. Your suffering has saved us. I love you.

To learn more about WaterBrook Press and view our catalog of products, log on to our Web site: **www.waterbrookpress.com**

WATERBROOK
PRESS